Epic Fails in Ancient History

Uncovering Hilarious Mistakes and Baffling Blunders That Shaped Civilizations

Welcome Aboard, Check Out This Limited-Time Free Bonus!

Ahoy, reader! Welcome to the Ahoy Publications family, and thanks for snagging a copy of this book! Since you've chosen to join us on this journey, we'd like to offer you something special.

Check out the link below for a FREE e-book filled with delightful facts about American History.

But that's not all - you'll also have access to our exclusive email list with even more free e-books and insider knowledge. Well, what are ye waiting for? Click the link below to join and set sail toward exciting adventures in American History.

Access your bonus here!

https://ahoypublications.com/

Or, Scan the QR Code!

Thanks for your support!

Table of Contents

Introduction

Learning about the history of your ancestors and bearing witness to all the discoveries, innovations, artworks, and knowledge they left behind is awe-inspiring. Knowing that they accomplished all they did with the little technology and facilitating resources at the time makes you realize just how powerful, creative, and capable humans can be. It is unfathomable how they also made mistakes and that some of the greatness that still stands today, whether in the form of monuments, artifacts, or information, might have been a product of what was considered an epic fail.

The grandeur of the past and the tales and events that historic temples, objects, and scriptures beheld throughout their lifetimes are captivating. Knowing that you're walking through the same halls that one of the most popular kings in history once wandered through, delving into the triumphs of age-old civilizations, and reading telltales that people made up to better understand the world around them are all surreal experiences. What's even more astounding is realizing that the quirks and imperfections of human nature are nestled within all this brilliance.

This book will teach you about history's greatest figures' missteps, failures, and errors. This is not to disparage these legends but to add a human touch to their experiences. It further shows their persistence to achieve greatness despite their failures, which is nothing short of inspiring. You'll not only feel motivated, but you'll also feel more connected to the past. You'll somewhat be able to relate to humans you probably once thought to be extraordinary.

This book, unlike other historical reads, aims to demystify the past. It doesn't lay out the insurmountable achievements in history but takes an unexpected, fresh detour from the anticipated storylines. Unless you are familiar with the incidents explored in this book, you'll never be able to guess what happens next. This element of surprise and unpredictability makes it different from similar books on the market. In other words, you don't have to be a history enthusiast to enjoy this read, and even if you're an avid reader of history, you'll likely find at least a few events you never knew about.

As you flip through the pages, you will grow more intrigued with the flaw-ridden tales, from the peculiar architectural mishaps of ancient Egypt to the ancient Chinese emperor's pursuit of immortality. You will also find end-of-chapter questions that will prompt you to ponder the causes and implications of these moments in time.

Chapter 1: Stone Age Stumbles

This opening chapter, based on events from thousands of years ago, aims to take you back to the early days of human civilization, unearthing the quirks and blunders that characterized our Stone Age ancestors. Starting with the puzzling case of Otzi, the Iceman, whose unforeseen demise was in the Alps, the chapter's stories offer a treasure trove of missteps and lessons in survival and conflict. Then, shifting focus to the Lascaux cave in France, the subsequent account examines the inadvertent threats posed by modern interventions that endangered ancient artworks. Finally, the last narrative dives into the intriguing discovery of Homo floresiensis, affectionately named "the hobbit," underlining initial misinterpretations and the mysteries surrounding this unique species.

Otzi, the Iceman

Otzi, the iceman.

On September 19, 1991, near the Ötztal Valley in Austria, a German couple stumbled upon what they thought was the remains of a victim of a mountaineering accident. The body was found buried from the waist down and lying face down. After reporting the body to the Similaun mountain refuge landlord, who notified both the Austrian and Italian police (as the body was found on the border of the two countries), the rescuers attempted to recover the body. However, located over 10,000 feet above sea level and partially buried in ice, not to mention the unpredictable weather, this wasn't an easy feat. After only being able to free a strange instrument from beside the body, it was taken to the valley while the remains were covered with a plastic sheet by the refuge landlord, Markus Pirpamer. Two days later, two curious mountaineers, Reinhold Messner and Hans Kammerlander, visited the site, and while looking at the leather clothing of the mummified remains, they began to suspect that the body was much older than initially thought. However, no archeologists were called, and after finally digging around the remains with icepicks and freeing it from its ice prison, the body was transported to Vent by a forensic scientist from Innsbruck. While removing the mummified remains from the ice, rescuers also found several other items under it, including clumps of hay, strings, leather fragments, hide pieces, and a bow and a dagger. From Vent, the body was transported to the Institute of Forensic Medicine in Innsbruck in a simple wooden coffin. Only then did an expert historian, Konrad Spindler, examine the body, determining it to be over 4,000 years old. He also noted that while the body was naturally preserved in Alpine conditions, it started to decay immediately once removed from the high altitude. He advised placing it in a cold cell to preserve its condition.

Further investigation determined that the remains (named Otzi, the Icemen, given the location of its discovery) belonged to a short, approximately 46-year-old man who lived over 5,000 years ago in Neolithic Europe. He had brown hair and eyes and was left-handed. Otzi was hailing from a line of farmers who migrated to Europe through Turkey 8,000 to 6,000 years ago. His paternal genetic line was traced down to the modern-day Mediterranean regions.

Wearing leather leggings, shoes stuffed with wild grass, two coats made of goat and sheep hides, and a hat made from bear fur, Otzi sat down for his last meal just a few hours before his death. After a long journey through the Ötztal Alps with a deerskin quiver, a wood-framed backpack, and a flint dagger, Otzi built a fire with the help of a birch bark receptacle containing the smoldering charcoal enveloped in maple leaves. He placed his copper axe beside him and had a filling meal of ibex, red deer meat, and einkorn wheat.

Otzi was tired not only because of the numerous conditions he struggled with (including intestinal parasites, cavities, heart disease, Lyme disease, arteriosclerosis, and back, knee, hip, and shoulder problems) but because he had a weakened state due to severe malnutrition –likely suffered in his final months – but also because he was severely injured.

He had been stabbed in his right hand between his first finger and thumb days before his death, which, given his left-handedness, clearly shows he was trying to defend himself from attackers. Unfortunately, before his wound had a chance to heal, he was struck by an arrow on the top of his left shoulder, which severed a major artery, causing him to bleed to death. He also had bleeding in his brain and was possibly hit in his head, too, but this hasn't been proven.

After spending some time at 8,200 feet, about 33 hours before his death, he descended to 4,000 feet to collect pollen and hunt, and at around 9 to 12 hours before his demise, he climbed up to where he was found and likely encountered someone who was after his bounty. With only two arrows in his quiver that normally held 20, Otzi was caught off guard, unable to defend himself.

Since his death occurred during the summer, Otzi's remains were likely mummified by the slightly warmer winds, which efficiently dried him out. Coupled with the icy temperatures that helped freeze his organs, the wind helped preserve his corpse, which then became the most studied human body in the world, not to mention a testimony to incredible human strength when facing adverse conditions. Moreover, scientists are still puzzled not only by the circumstances of his death but also by the extraordinarily harsh life Otzi had in the Alps – and his discovery and initial missteps in handling his body make studying his life and death even more challenging.

The Story of the Lascaux Cave in France

In 1940, Near Montignac, France, four teenagers chasing a dog through a narrow entrance into a cavern suddenly found themselves in front of a magnificent picture. While they were initially driven to follow the dog because of a local legend about a secret tunnel that promised to lead to a treasure, what they found was way beyond their imagination. After going through a narrow shaft leading down 50ft, they stood in a cave adorned with 15,000- to 17,000-year-old Upper Paleolithic paintings of animals. While initially apprehensive of what they would find, the picture of these ancient paintings bringing animals to life (almost as if they were moving) fascinated the boys, and they weren't the only ones.

The Lascaux cave had drawings of animals that brought them to life.
https://commons.wikimedia.org/wiki/File:Lascaux_painting.jpg

After climbing back up again, the boys told a few of their classmates about the caves with the paintings (leading them there in exchange for a small fee) and started a rumor that eventually made it to their schoolmaster, Leon Laval. Being an avid history buff, Laval was interested in this cave. Everything was talked about, but when the boys wanted to show him where it was located, he initially thought they wanted to trap him. However, after going down the same route the boys did a few days earlier, he discovered the site he immediately knew was of tremendous historical significance. Laval declared that from then on, no one should be allowed to go down, much less touch the paintings, wanting to preserve them from vandalism. One of the boys who discovered the cave agreed to stand guard (a commitment he held until he died in 1989).

When French archeologist and prehistorian Henri-Édouard-Prosper Breuil heard about the discovery, he immediately traveled to the site. After investigating nearly 1,500 engravings and 600 drawn and painted symbols and animals adorning the 16-foot-high and 66-foot-wide cavern (now known as the main cavern), he immediately declared them authentically prehistoric. As the news of the cave's discovery outgrew France and traveled across Europe, the owners of the cave's land started organizing daily tours in 1948, opening the grotto to thousands of annual visitors. Everyone who heard about the prehistoric paintings depicting animals in such detail, which put modern artists and illustrators to shame, wanted to see them.

Besides horses, cats, deer, bovines, and stags, the pictures also illustrate several mythical beings and a bird-headed person (the only human among all the shapes), which is believed to be a religious practice akin to shamans in later civilizations. Archeologists claim that the site was likely used for religious practices related to and detailing the hunting prowess of the locals. Some paintings have been linked to the constellation of Taurus and Pleiades, along with dancing (another indication of ritualistic events). When combined, the two associations indicate that participants of these religious ceremonies experienced trances and visions.

Further investigation of the cave led to the discovery of several side galleries adorned with animals and mythical creatures. They, alongside the main cavern paintings, depict the lives of the ancestors who lived around 15,000 B.C., dedicating their lives to art, religion, and even occult practices. Some of the pictures highlight burial practices, which convey that they believed in the afterlife and possibly an all-encompassing source of life (depicted as the mother goddess). They believed in mysterious forces that went beyond normal human experiences.

Many of the animals shown in the Lascaux cave paintings are extinct, but their hunters have successfully preserved their likeness forever, which was almost hindered by a huge blunder. When the owners opened the cave to the masses, they didn't consider how the growing traffic would affect the environment. They set up high-powered lights to make the painting visible from all angles, giving the best possible experience to the paying visitors but fading the artwork in the process. And, as those thousands of visitors got closer to observe the paintings, they breathed on them, creating condensation. As the moisture began to collect on the ceilings and walls, mold and lichen started to thrive, doing even more damage to the paintings. At one point, the air became so thick that visitors started to faint after spending only a few minutes inside. Possibly because of the newfound health hazard rather than to preserve the paintings, André Malraux, the French minister of culture, finally ordered the site to be closed to the public in 1963. From then on, only historians were allowed into the Lascaux cave. The public had to wait 20 years to enjoy the sight again, albeit in a replica built near the original grotto. While the new site continues to fascinate people, the efforts to prevent the original artwork from further decaying also persist. After bringing together almost 300 historians and restoration experts from around the world in 2009, the French Ministry of Culture published numerous recommendations to halt the deterioration of the paintings. However, the initial misstep that led to the fading and mold-laden state of the pictures was never addressed.

Homo Floresiensis, the Hobbit

In 2001, a team of archeologists led by Raden Soejono and Mike Morwood, looking to trace ancient travel routes between Asia and Australia, started excavating in Liang Bua – a large, chilly cave about 1,600 feet above sea level in Flores, Indonesia, The site is located between two rivers, has a high roof that isolates it from the environment, plenty of natural resources for human habitation, and stone artifacts, which made the researchers believe that they would find proof of ancient travelers stopping and spending time there.

Even the first finding exceeded the team's expectations, including bones of rats, giant storks, Komodo dragons, Stegodons (primitive elephant species), and other exotic animals. However, the most spectacular discovery was made on September 2, 2003, when diggers unearthed a very unusual-looking skull. It was identified as a human skull, but it was much smaller than the team had expected to find in the Pleistocene layer they were excavating at the time. The bones (both the skull and the rest of the body found under) were also very fragile, and because of this, the team decided to cut them out, along with the surrounding sediment – painstaking work that took several days.

Upon examining the small remains, the team quickly concluded that they belonged to a child. However, the scientists responsible for the bones' faunal identification disagreed, claiming they belonged to another species and not that of modern humans. Faced with the dilemma of identifying the remains, team leaders asked paleoanthropologist Peter Brown to join them at the site in Indonesia. Before arriving, Brown recalls expecting to find either the bones of a child (as initially claimed) or that of a person suffering from a genetic or other pathological condition that stunted their growth. Not trusting the judgment and experience of the original team, Brown was skeptical about the finding of a new human species. However, he immediately confirmed that they belonged to a different species after looking at the few cleaned skull pieces.

Upon reconstructing the skull, the team found that its owner had a brain capacity of less than a third of the brain capacity of modern humans. This left them flabbergasted because up until that time, it was believed that hominins with a brain this small lived 2.5 to 3 million years ago, which is much earlier than the layer of the sediments they found the bones in were formed. The bones were soon carbon-dated, confirming that they were approximately 18,000 years old, which coincided with the timeline the team was originally looking at – the late Pleistocene. It was also determined that the bones belonged to a 3-foot-tall primitive hominin female.

Further (still mistaken) theories claimed that the newfound species were the descendants of Homo Erectus – the early hominin species that lived on Java (very close to the site where the bones were located) until 150,000 years ago. This theory was supported by the belief that because the descendants of Homo Erectus lived there until the tail end of the last Ice Age, they adapted to the limited resources by shrinking in size. According to another theory, the new species was rather more likely a distant relation to the australopithecines, which lived in Africa over 2 million years ago and had similarly small features.

Despite being unable to pinpoint these new species' origins, the original research team finally brought their discovery into the public light in 2004. They announced their findings as a small offshoot of modern humans.

Initially, the species was given the name Sinanthropus floresianus (which translates as the "man from the Sunda region in Flores," but was soon renamed Homo floresiensis, as everyone agreed it was a member of the Homo genus. To raise public awareness (because they still needed other experts to confirm the findings) of the discovery and because the official Latin name was too difficult to pronounce, Mike Morwood and his colleagues also gave another name to the new species, "hobbit."

Partially because of this unusual nickname, the news of its discovery grabbed public attention immediately. Many in the scientific community questioned the veracity of the findings, finding it preposterous to believe that hominins could have evolved separately in South Asia and persisted until the late Pleistocene.

After reading the news article published in Nature magazine on October 28, 2004, some paleoanthropologists still believed that the remains belonged to a pathological skeleton, citing microcephaly when comparing the publicized measurements of the skull to other small-brained skulls they encountered during their previous findings.

At one point, the bones were taken by Teuku Jacob, who tried to take molds of the skull – which could've easily destroyed it due to its fragility. Immediately after the first attempt, the lower jaw broke. Eventually, the bones were returned to Indonesia, and more and more experts kept confirming they belonged to a new species. Instead of an outer mold, an endocast was made (the inner cast made of a hollow object), which revealed that the hobbit's brain might have been small, but it resembled more of the Homo Erectus brain than the endocast from primitive humans with small brains. The endocasts were also compared to the brains of skulls with confirmed microcephaly. Finding no similarities between them, this theory was finally put to rest, although the findings opened a discussion of other possible causes, including Laron syndrome and Down syndrome.

After examining the feet, scientists also started to argue that because of their anatomy and because of the large animals that lived in that area during the species' lifetime, they were most likely climbers that lived in trees.

With research continuing in Liang Bua, scientists hope to find answers to numerous questions, including whether the hobbit's lifetime overlapped with the appearance of modern humans in the area.

Not only did the discovery of this new species put Southeast Asia at the forefront of research into human evolution, but it also shook up previously established beliefs, including that the only two species that existed around the same time were modern humans and the Neanderthals. In fact, the entire reason why the team that discovered the hobbit began the excavation in Southeast Asia was that they believed they would find remains belonging to *modern humans.* Instead, they found what became one of the most important discoveries regarding human evolution. The line of the hobbit might have been a dead end evolution-wise, but its discovery put everything into a different perspective, changing how scientists think about evolutionary facts.

End of Chapter Questions

Here are a few questions to reflect on after reading this chapter:

1. How did modern interventions at the Lascaux cave paradoxically pose a risk to preserving ancient history?

2. What can the final moments and belongings of Otzi, the Iceman, tell us about the lifestyle and challenges people of his era faced?

3. Why was the discovery of Homo floresiensis initially met with skepticism, and what factors contributed to its eventual acceptance in the anthropological community?

Fun Facts

- Despite being over 5,000 years old, Otzi has 19 living relatives in Austria today, as found through DNA analysis!
- While famous for their meticulous animal depictions, the Lascaux cave paintings don't include images of the surrounding landscape and sky – a prominent feature in later historical art.
- While Homo floresiensis was publicly nicknamed "hobbit" due to its extremely small stature, its skull was originally thought to be that of a small child, not a fully-grown adult!

Chapter 2: Egyptian Errors

This chapter delves into incredibly fascinating errors in ancient Egyptian history. Errors in Snefru's commissioned pyramid, Akhenaten's ruling strategies, and the placement of Tutankhamun's tomb essentially led to greatness. This chapter proves that what are often perceived as life-altering mistakes are the keys to positive transformation and success. This intriguing yet highly peculiar read will take you through the annals of pharaonic history, from the innovative pyramid-building techniques to the art of tomb creation and placement.

Architectural Anomaly of Snefru's Bent Pyramid

Sneferu: The Innovative Pyramid Commissioner

The ancient Egyptian king, Sneferu, rose to power in the 25th century BCE. He was the first ruler of the 4th Egyptian dynasty and secured his kingship by marrying into the royal bloodline. During his reign, Sneferu led several raids toward Nubia and Libya. He also commanded excavations in the valley temple of one of his pyramids, leading to the revelation of the first record of Egypt's administrative and governmental system. His reign was generally believed to be a golden age.

King Sneferu was particularly interested in the construction of pyramids.

The king was particularly interested in expanding the nation and encouraging technical innovations, especially in the architecture and construction of pyramids. The three major pyramids he built are the Bent and Red pyramids at Dahshur, an ancient Egyptian necropolis and pyramid complex, and the Meidum pyramid at Meidum, which is an archeological site in lower Egypt. It's also worth noting that Snefru's descendants were the ones responsible for the three renowned pyramids of Giza: Khufu's pyramid (Snefru's son), Khafre's pyramid (Khufu's son), and Menkaure's pyramid (Khafre's son).

While Snefru's successors commissioned building pyramids that are now among the most popular wonders of the world, Snefru's innovative pyramids were significantly larger than those commissioned by his predecessors. He was also responsible for transitioning from creating the pyramids in the form of steps to making them flat-sided.

The Meidum was initially built as a step pyramid. However, the king later ordered its modification to make it appear more flat-sided. The Bent Pyramid, his second commission, is the first true pyramid ever built. A few years later, he commissioned the construction of the Red Pyramid, where he was later buried. While the Meidum mostly collapsed, the other two still stand today.

The Bent Pyramid

The Bent Pyramid is among the most unique of the 118 pyramids found in Egypt. While most of these pyramids are either stepped or flat-sided, Snefru's creation is oddly sloped. Around two-thirds of the height of the pyramid's sides are slightly sloped, while the rest of its length takes an extreme angle. Amazingly, it is also one of the only five pyramids that retained its true form thousands of years later. The Bent Pyramid offers the greatest insight into ancient Egyptians' architectural and construction techniques because of its unique shape and how it marks the transition from stepped to true pyramids.

Snefru's bent pyramid.
Julian Wishahi, CC BY-NC-SA 2.0 DEED <https://creativecommons.org/licenses/by-nc-sa/2.0/>
https://www.flickr.com/photos/121476474@N04/26905186026

The architectural landmark is constructed with white limestone and stands at around 343.5 feet tall. The slope of the lower part of the pyramid is 55°, and the upper part is angled at 43°. The valley temple comprises three sections: one of them has storerooms and is decorated with images of scenes from mortuary estates, another section is adorned with funerary estates, and the last section in the northern part of the temple contains ten limestone, red-colored columns with depictions of Sneferu engaging in certain rituals.

The valley temple, which accommodated priests believed to be a part of the ruler's mortuary cult, is enclosed by a huge mudbrick wall. The pyramid complex was also surrounded by a large limestone wall, creating a courtyard around the pyramid. Sneferu gave several pointers to the engineers throughout the construction of the bent pyramid. At first, it was constructed at 60° before it was reduced to 55°. Sneferu also demanded that the pyramid feature a larger base.

Although its engineers had already started building steep sides for it, Sneferu ordered them to make the pyramid more angled (45°), which resulted in its bent appearance. The engineers also realized that using the old stone-laying method with the newly developed inward-sloping building technique would cause stress to build up within the structure; they had to develop a new way to do it.

There are two entrances to the Pyramid's substructure. One of them serves as a corridor that leads to an underground antechamber that takes you to a burial chamber, which houses Snefru's engraved scroll, and the other is a corridor that leads to an upper chamber with limestone masonry.

Why Is It Bent?

Aside from Snefru's desire to transform the way pyramids were built, several theories regarding the appearance of the bent pyramid emerged. Some scholars believe that the king experienced an unexpected death, causing constructors to rush through the completion of the temple. Others believe that the engineers would've maintained the initial angle of the sides of the pyramid if it hadn't been for sounds and echoes emerging from the interior, cluing them to the fact that the angle wasn't sustainable.

Many archeologists also suggest that both the Bent and the Red pyramids were completed simultaneously, symbolizing Snefru's role as the double-king. He ruled over the North, represented by a red crown, and the South, represented by a white one. Another theory suggests that the Bent Pyramid intentionally takes this odd form to align astronomically with cosmic laws and rituals that the king's sun cult believed in. Some believe that Sneferu also commissioned the Meidum to be a sloped pyramid. However, the temple collapsed while the Bent Pyramid was still being built, urging engineers to rethink their building techniques and calculations in order to make the latter a more sustainable structure.

Regardless of whether Snefru had actually commissioned engineers to create a bent pyramid or if its peculiar form was a result of unfortunate events and revelations, this temple is considered among the most outstanding technical and architectural breakthroughs of its time. It radicalized the construction of successive ancient Egyptian royal tombs in shape, size, and building material.

The Bent Pyramid is made of substantially heavier and larger stone blocks than the ones used for preceding monuments. Therefore, constructors had to exchange their building techniques for methods that would suit the new material. While earlier pyramid-building techniques didn't differentiate between the external layer of the temple and its casting, the architects of the Bent Pyramid had to use casting blocks to create a flat exterior.

Specialists suggest that they tried to fill in the steps in the Meidum Pyramid using the same technique. However, they went wrong by placing the casting blocks horizontally before cutting the sloped edges off. They cut the castings into rectangular blocks to avoid another collapsed monument before laying them at inward-sloping 17° angles. While it was significantly more difficult to do, this method strengthened the structure by leveraging gravity. It pulls its mass inward and downward toward the earth.

Religious Revolution of Pharaoh Akhenaten

Akhenaten, Tutankhamun's father, rose to power during the 18th century. His reign lasted for nearly two decades, and he was known for radicalizing ancient Egyptian religion. The king was also popular for being a connoisseur and innovator of the arts. That said, his kingship led to a period of turmoil and unrest.

Akhenaten's reign lasted nearly two decades.

The king was born around 1370 BC and was brought up in rich, powerful, and prosperous ancient Egypt. Akhenaten grew up learning about ancient Egyptian traditional religion and literature, and he served in the military. At the time of his upbringing, the Theban priests of Amun were among the highest-ranking individuals in the societal and governmental system. They enjoyed abundant wealth and high social status and were even considered the foes of the pharaohs.

Born Amenhotep IV, Akhenaton served as his father's co-regent for several years before he qualified as king. While this briefing period was likely scheduled to last longer, Akhenaten had to step into power at just 16 years old following his father's abrupt death. At the beginning of his reign, the newly-appointed king did nothing out of the ordinary. He worshipped the traditional god Amun and maintained the customary guidelines of kingship.

The Rise of Atenism

Half a decade into his rule, however, Amenhotep IV started promoting controversial ideologies. He claimed that Aten, a sun deity, was the sole, true god and urged people to worship him alone. These beliefs are what led him to rebrand himself as "Akhenaten," which translates to "the servant of Aten." Akhenaten didn't merely suggest that people embrace his new faith but outlawed the worship of any other deity. He shut down any temple that didn't belong to Aten and got rid of all representations of the other deities.

Naturally, his forceful ways and his eccentric views weren't well-received by the public at the time. Most people accused him of betraying ancient Egypt's cultures, traditions, and religious systems. His denunciation of all the other gods also resulted in the lost influence and relevance of the once potent priests of Amun, leading to political uproar.

The king also created a new city and called it Akhetaten (now known as Amarna), which translates to the "Horizon of Aten," and he named it the new capital instead of Thebes. The city accommodated several temples dedicated to Aten. He designed it in a way that all temples faced east, toward the direction of the rising sun, in honor of the deity.

Internal and Diplomatic Trouble

The conflict that Akhenaten's rule sparked traveled beyond the borders of ancient Egypt. He was met with extreme backlash and opposition from the people and the priests who dedicated their lives to other gods. Even the priests of Amun were forced to abandon their old beliefs and dedicate their priesthood to Aten.

The king was also largely concerned with building Akhetaten – instead of redirecting his efforts and resources into expanding the empire. His lack of focus on military and governmental affairs hindered diplomatic relationships with the surrounding rulers. Archeologists found letters at Amarna that proved Akhenaten's neglect of diplomatic affairs and his shameless requests for material gifts and resources.

The Great Royal Wife

Nefertiti, whom Akhenaten married, played an incredible role as a co-ruler of ancient Egypt. She helped transform the society and religious system alongside Akhenaten and was seen as his female equivalent. She was depicted with her husband more than any other queen and was titled the "Great Royal Wife." She was also shown making sacrifices to Aten without Akhenaten, which signals the great amount of power she held in court. Nefertiti was portrayed victoriously fighting the enemies of ancient Egypt, which was a depiction reserved only for the kings. The queen also had her own temple at Akhetaten. Scholars suggest that she ruled the country after Akhenaten's death.

Changes in Art

The shift from polytheism to monotheism caused artists to change how they did art. They had to abandon their traditional depictions of the gods and pharaohs and create artworks of scenes from everyday life instead. Even depictions of the royal family were done through a more realistic lens. This change in art may have also been influenced by the Atenism belief that Aten was found in everything in the world. Art at the time also frequently incorporated the sun disk, which is a symbol of Aten.

Akhenaten's Death and What Followed

Scholars suggest that Akhenaten started growing ill around 12 years into his rule, leading to his death five years later. Others suggest that he was murdered in the 17th year of his kingship. As one would expect, his religious reformations didn't last long after he died. When his son, Tutankhaten, took over, he changed his name to Tutankhamun, reopened the temples his father shut down, and brought back the traditional worship of Amun. He also renamed Thebes as the ancient Egyptian capital.

The ancient Egyptians tried their best to erase all memories of Amun and his tumultuous reign. They got rid of his name from public monuments and destroyed images and depictions of him. Their efforts were so successful that no proof of Akhenaten's existence was discovered until the 19th century when Amarna was rediscovered and the king's tomb was excavated.

The Peculiarities of Tutankhamun's Tomb

King Tutankhamun was only nine years old when he rose to power. He was guided and advised by professional visors until he was capable. Although his rule was short-lived due to his premature death, he left a significant mark in Egypt's history. The idea of a child ruling over one of the most complex, powerful, and magnificent empires of the time is deeply intriguing.

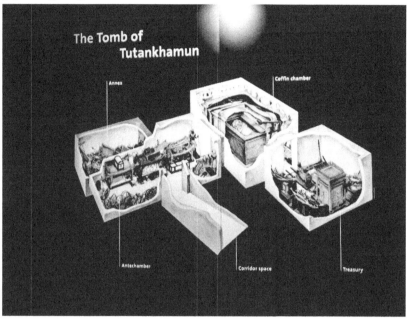

The layout of Tutankhamun's tomb.
Mary Harrsch, CC BY-NC-SA 2.0 DEED < https://creativecommons.org/licenses/by-nc-sa/2.0/ >
https://www.flickr.com/photos/mharrsch/33049813133

The world-renowned king died at only 18 or 19 years old, which further contributes to the mystical air surrounding him. His cause of death is still a popular subject of debate among field professionals. While early examinations suggested that the king suffered a blow to the head, modern-day CT scans and DNA analysis revealed that he might've been engaged in a chariot accident or struggled with malaria or degenerative bone disease.

Egyptologists agree that Tutankhamun's tomb preparation was rushed as it wasn't like the elaborately planned tombs of the other kings, which often took years to prepare. It seems to be covered with incomplete decorations, smaller than usual, and supplemented with reused artifacts.

His burial process was also hastened, and inadequate details regarding his death were recorded, which is probably due to his unexpected death. Many suggest that the tomb was initially meant for someone else but ended up being used for King Tut. Even his grave goods seem to be randomly selected and out of place.

The Odd Placement of the Tomb

Most kings were buried at the Valley of the Kings. However, King Tutankhamun's resting place was oddly situated within it. The king's tomb was hidden beneath the entrance of Ramses VI's tomb. Its peculiar placement and small size caused it to go unnoticed for thousands of years. Many people believe that it was an uncalculated decision driven by the king's unexpected death, while others believe it was done intentionally to protect the sarcophagus. After all, the tomb is among the most exquisite and valuable artifacts in history. It is made of 110 kg of pure gold and features a detailed carving of the pharaoh. Whether it was intended or not, the hidden location of the tomb protected it against the damaging effects of time and the greed of intruders.

Tutankhamun's grave was oddly placed close to the entrance of Rameses VI's tomb.
Elias Rovielo, CC BY-NC-SA 2.0 DEED <https://creativecommons.org/licenses/by-nc-sa/2.0/>
https://www.flickr.com/photos/eliasroviello/44060676590

The Fascinating Grave Goods

Tutankhamun's grave included a collection of over 5,000 goods. The objects range from daily-use items, such as loincloths and self-care equipment, to symbolic items used in rituals. Highly personal and sentimental items, such as his mummified stillborn daughters and a lock of his grandmother's hair, were also found in the grave. Wine, dates, lentils, and other foods and beverages were also found.

The king's grave goods also included tools like chisels and cubit rods and weapons such as bows and arrows, chariots, and armor. Luxurious objects like staffs and headrests made of precious metals, linen gloves, Libyan jewels, and Nubian ivory and ebony were also found. Egyptologists also discovered sandals, makeup, pieces of furniture, and even board games in the grave. These objects offered a lot of insight into the nation's diplomatic affairs and the everyday life of ancient Egypt at the time.

The Sound of History

Interestingly, King Tut's tomb was home to the only surviving trumpet from ancient Egypt. This artifact is the oldest musical instrument in the world. As one would expect, it was crafted from silver and gold. Not only is the elaborate piece beautiful to look at, but it's extremely astounding to listen to as well. It's a once-in-a-lifetime opportunity to listen to the sounds of history. After being silent for over three millennia, bandsman James Tappern of Prince Albert's Own 11th Royal Hussars regiment played the instrument in 1939 in front of the Egyptian Museum. Late research suggests that the instrument was used for military purposes rather than entertainment.

From the peculiar build of the still-standing Bent Pyramid to the ornate playable trumpet, this chapter is a testament to ancient Egyptian greatness. Even their errors led to groundbreaking innovations and discoveries. The Bent Pyramid, the religious transformations of Akhenaten and his reign, and the peculiarities of Tutankhamun's tomb shed light on the skills, way of thinking, and lifestyle of those who inhabited the Cradle of Civilization thousands of years ago.

End of Chapter Questions

Here are a few questions to reflect on after reading this chapter:

1. How did the design flaws in Snefru's Bent Pyramid reflect the evolving understanding of pyramid construction during ancient Egyptian times?

2. Considering ancient Egypt's rich pantheon of gods, why did Akhenaten's shift to monotheism face such strong resistance and quick reversal after his reign?

3. What anomalies in King Tutankhamun's tomb suggest it might not have been the originally intended resting place for the young pharaoh?

Fun Facts

• Despite the apparent "error" in its design, Snefru's Bent Pyramid is unique and is one of the best-preserved pyramids from ancient Egypt, retaining much of its smooth limestone casing.

• Akhenaten and his wife, Nefertiti, are often depicted in art with elongated skulls, leading to numerous speculations and theories, including extraterrestrial origins!

• While King Tutankhamun is one of the most well-known pharaohs globally, his reign was relatively short and historically uneventful; the discovery of his nearly intact tomb in 1922 catapulted him to international fame.

Chapter 3: Greek Gaffes

Honing in on the lives of the Ancient Greeks and the mishaps that shaped their civilization, the chapter begins with the story of the Sicilian Expedition during the Peloponnesian War, showcasing this fatal military campaign as one of the Greeks' disastrous attempts to conquer the shores of Europe. The second story dives into a somewhat humorous yet equally tragic event involving a bird and a tortoise that led to the death of the renowned Greek playwright, Aeschylus. Concluding the chapter, the last story examines the shocking arson of Herostratus, a man who destroyed the magnificent Temple of Artemis in search of fame and fortune.

The Sicilian Expedition and the Peloponnesian War

Led by Athens' enormous military power, the Delian League (formed by a union of Greek cities after the Persian War) set out to fight back the Persian invasion and Sparta. On the other hand, the Spartans were more concerned about the incredible speed with which Athens was obtaining more and more power in the region. In an attempt to regain control of the economic and military power, the Spartans started engaging the Athenians in a series of conflicts, eventually leading to the Peloponnesian War. After achieving a massive victory and taking 292 Spartan captives during the Battles of Pylos and Sphacteria, in 425 BC, Athens gained a major advantage, and the Spartans' powers were dwindling. However, somewhere in the next three years, the tides turned, and suddenly, Athens was on the losing side.

In 422 BC, after losing key leaders and being exhausted and afraid of losing allies, both sides needed time to regroup and recoup their losses. Their clash over dominance was briefly put on hold by the Peace of Nicias in 421 BC, although this period of calm was short-lived, which was partially because of the Athenians' epic failure to realize they had been duped. Signed by King Pleistoanax on the Spartan and Commander Nicias on the Athenian side, this treaty of eighteen clauses seemingly promised both sides a peaceful resolution. Prisoners were exchanged, control over major cities was returned to the other, and mutual support was guaranteed for future third-party attacks. However, in a bafflingly clever maneuver, the Spartans sneaked in a clause that provided them a loophole against going through with a promise the Athenians counted on. Namely, the Spartans pledged to restore Amphipolis in the same treaty, which they never intended to do as it would have given the Athenians too much power. When the time came to begin the restoration, the Athenians realized their mistake, but it was too late. However, now they were (rightfully) suspicious of the Spartans, and as the mistrust grew, the peace intended to last for half a century was over after only a handful of years.

The mistrust was transferred to the allies of both sides, including Athen's Sicilian allies. In 415 BC, the Sicilian forces supporting Athens were besieged by the Syracusans, who, in turn, allied with the Spartans. As a response, Athens launched the Sicilian Expedition as a counterattack on the Syracusans, which many argue contributed to the continuation of the war. The Spartans were slighted by Athens' actions because they doubted the Athenians' claims that they were only trying to defend their allies. And they had every reason to do so.

Initially, Athens' forces were led by several powerful military officers, including Commander Nicias, who favored peace and had previously signed the treaty, and General Alcibiades, who took a more aggressive approach to the Athenian leadership. Alcibiades was determined not to make the same mistake as Nicias and trust the Spartans. He thought it best to destroy the Spartan allies (and thus weaken the Spartan power), and despite Nicias's disapproval, Alcibiades gathered a troop of 5,000 infantrymen and more than 100 ships and was ready to set on the journey to aid Athens' Sicilian allies at Syracuse. At least, this was the official plan. Alcibiades's true plan was much more insidious and, as it turned out, overreaching. Alcibiades secretly hoped that with the force he now possessed, he could conquer the city of Syracuse, expanding the Athenian resources and control in the region (while taking something away from the Spartans). However, a few religious monuments in Athens were mysteriously damaged just before his departure. Given his previous fame of aggression and disapproval of religion, Alcibiades was inoculated for this crime, forcing his fleet to depart to Sicily without him.

Alcibiades's absence from the frontline of the Sicilian expedition notwithstanding, the Athenians had much bigger problems to contend with. Sending such a massive force to Sicily was a huge mistake in the first place because if something went wrong and Athens was attacked by another party, there wouldn't be enough men to defend it. Moreover, after seeing their massive numbers arriving at the Sicilian shores, even their Sicilian supporters began to suspect that the Athenians didn't just arrive to help but to conquer. This was their second mistake because this weakened the Sicilians' trust in them. The third one was to decide that since mistrust had already arisen, they might as well go ahead with their attempt to conquer. General Lamachus, who led the expedition in Alcibiades's absence, proposed that they launch an attack right after their arrival while the city was still unprepared. Nicias, however, was afraid that this attempt would backfire (which it did) and argued that they should simply support the allies as long as needed and then return home.

The next mistake on the Athenians' side was underestimating the Syracusan forces' reaction. As soon as the Athenians set up a base near Syracuse, Syracusan General Hermocrates began gathering allies from the anti-Athenian territories, including Corinth, Carthage, and Sparta. At first, the Athenians delivered several major blows, although they were far from winning the war. With Alcibiades awaiting trial in Athens, the two other Athenian commanders raided the northern shores of Sicily. Here, they made their next mistake. They sustained their troops by capturing small villages and selling the goods *and people* they found there, and cutting all ties with their former allies who couldn't stand beside these atrocious acts. Still, the Athenian troops marched on and even started the siege of Syracuse because, initially, Hermocrates could only convince a few of his allies to help reorganize the current Syracusan structure of command. Even more concerning to the Athenians, most of their allies either shifted sides or agreed to remain neutral but withdrew their support of Athens in the conflict. Yet, this still wasn't enough to stop them.

After General Lamachus was killed in the first battle, Nicias was left to fight against the Syracusans. Soon, he was faced with Gylippus, a powerful Spartan military adviser who came to the Syracusans' aid. Athenian reinforcement was also on the way, but it came way too late – only adding to the series of failures that marked this campaign. By the time General Demosthenes arrived with additional troops, the Athenian forces were already dwindling. In 413 BC, Athens's worst fear came true. Sparta had openly declared war against Athens, which meant the Athenians couldn't send additional reinforcement to Syracuse, sealing the fate of the Sicilian expedition. The mighty Athenian fleet Alcibiades – once believed to be able to conquer Syracuse – was slowly destroyed, and in a cruel twist of fate, the Athenian warriors who survived the battles in Sicily were taken captive and forced to work as slaves to those they once sought to enslave themselves.

Athens focused on the war against Sparta, which lasted almost another decade, but the Sicilian disaster put them at a serious disadvantage. Slowly but surely, their massive advantage was lost, along with their allies, and Athens was forced to surrender to Sparta in 404 BC. Along with the Peloponnesian War, the Golden Age of Greece was also over, as both the Spartans and the Athenians took decades to recover.

The Life and Death of Aeschylus

Aeschylus was a member of a wealthy and noble aristocratic family.
Tilemachos Efthimiadis, CC BY-SA 2.0 <https://creativecommons.org/licenses/by-sa/2.0>, via Wikimedia Commons: https://commons.wikimedia.org/wiki/File:Aeschylusathens.jpg

Born in the city of Eleusina (also known as Eleusis) in the 5th century, Aeschylus was a wealthy and noble aristocratic family member. The young Aeschylus tended to a vineyard in this town not far from Athens.

Aeschylus possessed a great deal of talent for drama, which is evident in how he explains the beginnings of his career. According to his story, after falling asleep after a hard day of work, Aeschylus received a message from Dionysus, the divine patron of winemakers. In this dream vision, Dionysus, the god of theater in ancient Greece, suggested that Aeschylus should explore the art of tragedy. While some claim that he was more likely inspired by the grapes and wine surrounding him rather than a deity, it doesn't matter. This vision marked the beginning of a career that made Aeschylus one of the most well-known poet-dramatists (sometimes referred to as the father of tragedy) of ancient Greece. The day after his dream, Aeschylus began writing his first tragedy and finished it soon after.

Around the time Aeschylus started writing tragedies, literacy contests were very popular in ancient Greece. In 484 BC, Aeschylus won his first competition at a famous Dionysian celebration. A few years later, during the Greco-Persian conflicts, his writing career was put on hold when he was summoned into military service. Aeschylus and his brother, Cynaegirus, participated in the Battle of Marathon, defending Athens against the army of Darius I of Persia, and the Battle of Salamis (known from his tragedy called The Persians).

Beyond being a poet and a war hero, Aeschylus was also a member of the secret Cult of Demeter, often partaking in the Eleusinian mysteries, the rites dedicated to the exploration of the connection between life and death. However, because he revealed cult secrets by incorporating ritualistic elements into his stage performances in these tragedies, Aeschylus faced trial and a possible death sentence. Fortunately, his outstanding military performance saved him from this fate, and he was acquitted after his trial. Later on, Aeschylus married and had two sons, one (Euphorion) of whom also became a poet.

Legends describe Aeschylus as a sensitive and superstitious person. For example, when he lost a literacy competition to a younger, upcoming writer (Sophocles) in 468 BC, Aeschylus was so upset that he departed for Sicily, where he soon became just as popular as he was in Athens. The king of this island often invited Aeschylus later on, encouraging him to create work there as well. One of the times he returned to Sicily was exactly after his acquittal upon the trial about the Eleusinian Mysteries, and it was on this island that this great poet met a tragic end in 455 BC.

Before his death, Aeschylus was warned by an oracle about the possible danger to his life. According to the legends, the poet was told that his death would be caused by a hard object falling onto his head. Thinking this would most likely be a building collapsing or an ornament falling from a ceiling, Aeschylus began to spend as little time indoors as possible. While he took the premonition seriously, unfortunately, his mistaken belief that he would be safer outdoors (and forgetting that things could fall on his head outside as well) cost him his life. One day, as Aeschylus was enjoying the great outdoors at Gela and contemplating his next work, an eagle dropped a tortoise onto his head (mistaking his bald cranium for a shiny rock), killing him in an instant.

The poet and magnificent warrior, whose life ended in this absurd manner, was never returned to Athens but was buried at Gela. Interestingly enough, his epitaph only talks about his glorious valor on the battlefields, not his talent for drama and tragedy. However, this wasn't unusual for the ancient Greeks, who emphasized celebrating those who fought for their country. Even in exile, Aeschylus's heroic accomplishments were never forgotten; being a great dramatist couldn't overshadow them.

Only after his death did Aeschylus receive accomplishment for his contribution to the art of drama and essentially founding the trilogy genre. While only seven of his works have fully survived the test of time, historians found the titles of up to 90 more possible plays he could have written during his lifetime. According to archeological evidence found in an ancient Egyptian papyrus, the seven works of Aeschylus were awarded numerous times, granting him 13 victories at the Dionysius celebrations.

Just as he is celebrated for his wartime accomplishment, Aeschylus also honored the heroes of his and previous eras. Laced with nationalism and patriotism, his work often centers around strong and noble heroes who make poetic speeches about defining the country and traditions. For example, the Oresteia trilogy, consisting of Eumenides, Agamemnon, and Choephori, details the intricate manner in which the family of the Argive King, Agamemnon, faced the dilemma of handling personal revenge while maintaining the foundations of public justice. Aeschylus also incorporated his personal military experience at the Battle of Salamis into his work, The Persians, which is considered one of the few pieces describing real-life events from ancient Greece.

Aeschylus is known for introducing many theatrical innovations, including more than one actor in dramas and receding the choir's role (which was previously massive, given it was the main participant besides the single actor). Due to this, the number of choir members was reduced as well, and Aeschylus personally chose and taught these members. Aeschylus was also the first to incorporate masks and costumes into his plays.

Herostratus and the Destruction of the Temple of Artemis

After settling on the shores of Ephesus (modern-day Turkey), Athenian colonists introduced their culture to the region. Central to their traditions was their worship of the goddess Artemis, the patron of hunters and wild animals and the goddess of childbirth. The Athenians erected a temple in her honor to solidify their reverence for this deity. At first, the stone temple was a simple place for worship, but after it was destroyed by a flood and the debris it carried, it was rebuilt in the 7th century BC. This time, it was transformed into a massive marble masterpiece, 150 feet wide and 377 feet long, supported by wooden beams, converting it into the largest Greek temple in the history of mankind. Its 127 columns were adorned with intricate designs, some of which were hand-carved by ancient Greece's most renowned artists. Further additions eluded the numerous massive statues of Artemis herself, with the largest one set in the middle of the temple under the partially closed roof. The Temple of Artemis became a gathering place for merchants, commoners, and noblemen. The new monument had a raised plateau, which was great for flood protection and forced public speeches. Its builders ensured that the temple would withstand natural disasters – what they didn't count on was destruction by the hands of a madman seeking power and fame.

Little is known about the background and early life of Herostratus. Some sources claim him to be a former slave, while others ensure he was a peasant. Either way, he was a heavily disgruntled man without status and wanted to change that. He thought if he set the largest temple in the region on fire, everyone in Ephesus would learn his name.

And they did.

Determined to obtain fame, on July 21, 356 BC, Herostratus walked into the Temple of Artemis, carrying tools for making a fire, including a tiny olive oil lamp and several rags he was able to conceal from the guards while entering the sanctuary. While Herostratus understood that he couldn't damage the marble facade, he was also aware of the vulnerability of the wooden elements, so he targeted those. He waited deep into the night until the place was empty, placed the oil-soaked rags around the wooden furnishing and beams, and set the wooden beams ablaze, starting from the inner sanctuary. As the pillars became engulfed in flames, they were unable to support the marble structure, which fell. Since part of the ceiling was also made of wood, along with a few of the statues of Artemis, by the next morning, these were in ashes, too. The 40-foot high columns were gone, leaving only the broken pieces of marble on the ground and the temple in ruins.

Herostratus burnt down the temple of Artemis.
https://commons.wikimedia.org/wiki/File:Temple_of_Artemis.jpg

Besides the smoldering remains, Herostratus waited for his capture and fame. He readily admitted the crime and his reasons for doing so. Instead of being ashamed of committing a horrendous act like this, he boasted about his achievement, believing it would be enough to make it into history. Herostratus was imprisoned and sentenced to death soon after, but Greek authorities were afraid that others would follow in his footsteps, wanting to obtain fame at any cost. To discourage acts like this, they implemented a new law that banned writing or speaking about condemned individuals, meaning whoever committed a crime like this again couldn't become famous. Those who broke this law faced the death penalty just like those committing the crimes. Despite this, the historian Theopompus made a detailed record of Herostratus's atrocious act, ultimately aiding the arsonist in his attempt to cement his name in history.

Theories about why Artemis herself allowed the arson to happen also arose among the locals. Some claimed the goddess was busy overseeing the birth of Alexander the Great, which coincidentally happened on the same night, so she failed to look over her temple. Later on, Alexander himself offered to finance the temple's reconstruction, but Ephesian officials refused, claiming one deity shouldn't build a place of worship for another and preferred to do the building themselves. Decades later, the Ephesians erected a third, even greater monument, which entered the history books as one of the Seven Wonders of the Ancient World. Half a millennia later, this temple was also destroyed by invaders. There were no more attempts to rebuild it afterward, and today, the magnificent Temple of Artemis is nothing more than a heap of rocks (albeit very popular among tourists). Another addition to history was the term "Herostratic fame," used on those who commit crimes seeking notoriety. The aforementioned term, Herostratus, and his arson were referenced by numerous artists, including famed authors like Cervantes and Chaucer.

The story of the Sicilian Expedition embodies Athens desperate attempts to gain back the tight military, economic, and political control they once had in the region. In stark contrast, the story of Aeschylus is simply the case of a person giving into their superstitions, setting aside the logical fact that things can fall from above the outside as well. The story of Herostratus is much like any modern story of an outrageous act of a person seeking attention at all costs.

End of Chapter Questions

Here are a few questions to reflect on after reading this chapter:

1. How did the failure of the Sicilian Expedition impact the broader context of the Peloponnesian War and Athens' political landscape?

2. While the story of Aeschylus' death is undoubtedly peculiar, what does it reveal about ancient Greek beliefs and views on fate?

3. Herostratus' desire for fame led him to commit an egregious act. How did ancient Ephesian society respond, and what measures did they take to deter similar future events?

Fun Facts

• The Peloponnesian War lasted for 27 years and wasn't an ongoing affair but was marked by temporary (and failed) attempts to achieve a truce and punctuated by surprising shifts in alliances.

• Some ancient sources imply that Aeschylus had been forewarned of his death by a prophecy stating he would be struck on his head by a falling object, prompting him to spend more time outdoors - ironically hastening his demise.

• The Temple of Artemis, one of the Seven Wonders of the Ancient World, was rebuilt after Herostratus' heinous act, but a subsequent invasion led to its destruction once again. Today, only a single column of the temple remains intact at the original site - the only testament to the magnificent splendor it once was.

Chapter 4: Roman Wrecks

The Roman Empire is one of the greatest imperial forces that the world has ever seen. At its height, Rome was the largest city in the world, with one million inhabitants, and the emperor's territory spanned two million square miles. From its beginning in 625 BC to its gradual fall and deterioration, leading up to its collapse in 476 AD, Rome went through numerous peaks and valleys. The historical mistakes of Rome have created many timeless moments and cultural mythologies that remain relevant to this day. Diving into Rome's mistakes reveals how societies adapt to adversity and innovate from defeat. Maintaining an empire for over a thousand years requires ingenuity to adapt to some civilization-shaking events along the way.

As much as Rome's military precision kept the empire together, its political prowess was what backed its deadly capabilities. Public spectacle and entertainment helped govern the people by instilling a cultural grandeur attached to the emperors and the marvels they facilitated. Rome's well-oiled public relations also had some hiccups in its overall greatness.

As the world's largest ancient city, Rome dealt with the growing pains of living in a densely populated area. The center of the ancient world experienced some disasters that led to unrest and, in many cases, innovation. Through the dance of success and failure, Rome was able to stand as a major superpower in the ancient world that still holds tons of historical relevance. The influence Rome has on the modern world cannot be denied, but in its majesty, Rome's mishaps are just as important to highlight. Some of Rome's blunders can be considered the beginning of the end, while others can be seen as those that propelled them into greatness. Explore this legendary empire through the lens of its biggest mistakes.

The Battle of the Teutoburg Forest

Early in the first century, Rome's military force was unrivaled around the world. Its sophisticated army not only had superior weapons technology, but its discipline and battlefield tactics made the entire globe shake in fear before the mighty imperial forces. Rome quickly expanded, conquering much of the world with precision and brutality. All the conquered lands assimilated as Roman citizens under the empire, paying taxes to the global political structure.

The Battle of Teutoburg Forest.
https://commons.wikimedia.org/wiki/File:Hermann (Arminius) at the battle of the Teutoburg Forest in 9 CE by Peter Janssen, 1873, with painting creases and damage removed.jpg

Rome's constant successes probably had its leaders feeling unstoppable. By the time the Battle of Teutoburg Forest was about to occur, the Romans had already conquered Celtic tribes in Northern and Central Europe, with the Rhine River acting as a border. The Roman Army was a powerful unit that was well-structured and almost undefeatable. The complex hierarchy system started with a legionary – an individual foot soldier. Eight legionaries formed a Contubernium.

Ten Contubernium made up a century, which consisted of 80 men. A cohort was six centuries, adding up to 480 men. To complete a legion of Roman soldiers, you needed at least ten cohorts, which would equal 4,800 men, with an additional 120 horsemen. The legion would be structured under a strict chain of command, with military leaders guiding soldiers from the frontlines.

This hierarchal structure, coupled with their superior technology, like their specially designed helmets, drove Rome to countless victories during its expansion. The flaw in the Roman army was yet unexploited at the time. Rome's strength was its ability to fight as a disciplined unit. Julius Caesar had conquered Gallia, which led to the region being divided into subjugated Celtic tribes and free Germanic cultures, which the Roman leadership considered uncivilized. Caesar Augustus trusted that his superior army could conquer the unorganized and un-unified Germanic tribes that dwelled east of the Rhine.

Legend has it that in 17 BC, the Sicambri tribe captured the standard eagle of Legion V Alaudae. The eagle was a beautifully crafted ornament that Roman legions carried to honor their gods, so losing it was a disgrace. Some say that this was part of the reason why Cesar Augustus was motivated to conquer the free Germanic tribes. They experienced some success with the surrender of Sicambri and the retrieval of the eagle, which stood as a great symbolic testament to Rome's imperial power. General Nero Claudius Druscus conquered a large section of land near the Rhine, which was dubbed Germania. Tiberius Julius took over command of the area when Druscus died. Emperor Augustus introduced an unpopular decree in the area, requiring the Germanic tribes to pay taxes to Rome, which understandably upset the locals.

Publius Quintictilius Varus governed Germania with the help of the eleven legions he commanded. The Germanic tribes had a revolutionary spirit but could not defeat their Roman conquerors due to a lack of unity and fighting among each other. This would all change with the rise of Arminius. As the son of Cheruscan Chieftain Segimerus, Arminius and his brother were captured when they were young boys as a tool to keep his father in check. Arminius was educated as a Roman and rose through their military ranks; however, he always harbored resentment for his Roman kidnappers regardless of his identity as a Roman citizen. Furthermore, he always felt a connection to his tribe, never forgetting where he came from.

Between 8 and 11 AD, an uprising occurred in the Balkans, leaving Varus with only three legions in the Rhine region. Due to his experience in the military, Arminius knew the weak spots he could target in the Roman fighting style. He worked to unite the tribes of Germania so they could ambush the Roman forces when they were most vulnerable. Arminius used some cunning tactics of deceit. He convinced his superiors of a fake rebellion that they needed to quell. A ten-mile-long Roman column with 20,000 soldiers marched through the woodland forest.

Mother Nature was not on the side of the Romans, battering them with wind, storms, and falling trees. The muddy surroundings greatly slowed down the Romans, who were ambushed in the forest. Arminius left under the false pretense that he was going to collect reconnaissance and recruit more troops for the mission. On the first day, the Romans were battered but managed to pull it together and set up camp. The next day, the Roman forces marched west toward military camps established in the area, but they were hundreds of miles away.

The Romans, who were now more prepared, managed to hold off their attackers on flatter terrain. By the third day, the Romans were forced to march through a narrow passage on the Kalkriese hill. The Germanic tribes had prepped the passage earlier, building walls to make the pass even thinner. The Romans were bombarded with spears and charging aggressors who thickened their ranks with constant reinforcements. The battle resulted in the loss of 20,000 soldiers. The men who didn't die in battle suffered a horrific fate. Survivors were tortured before being sacrificed to Germanic gods. Some tribal soldiers even collected body parts for the Romans as souvenirs of their miraculous victory.

The defeat in the Teutoburg forest lessened the respect of the Romans throughout the empire. Now, nations understood that defeating the once indestructible Roman army was possible. Arminius is still used as a symbol of liberation for some Germans. Roman historian Tacitus accounts how the battlefield of Kalkriese looked six years after the initial defeat. The bones lay scattered, with some being placed on alters. According to Tacitus, Arminius united many of the Germanic tribes until the jealousy and political ambitions of others caused the unification to fall apart, ending in his betrayal. The Romans eventually left Germania, solidifying the independence of Germanic tribes.

In the aftermath of the battle, Tiberius conquered many Germanic tribes but never went east of the Rhine, even when he became emperor. The leader eventually reconquered the Lippe Valley, along the coast of the North Sea, but still feared bringing Germanic tribes under Roman rule because of the great loss they had suffered. One of the most prominent legends attached to the event was recorded by the Historian Suetonius, who wrote that Emperor Augustus went into deep mourning, growing out his beard while crying out, "Quinctilius Varus, give me back my legions!"

Emperor Nero and the Great Fire of Rome

Emperor Nero Claudius Caesar is remembered as one of the most villainous figures in Rome. The emperor is often invoked when people point out the hedonistic debauchery of the Roman upper classes and political corruption at the highest levels. The Christianization of the West may be part of the reason why the Roman head is remembered so unfavorably, considering that he persecuted Christians and blamed them for one of the biggest failures of the empire, which was the Great Fire of Rome.

Emperor Nero is remembered as one of the most villainous figures in Rome.
https://commons.wikimedia.org/wiki/File:Rubens_-_Emperor_Nero,_d5334160g.jpg

Although Nero claimed that the fire was started by the Christians and some legends that later formed pointed out the emperor as the main suspect, the city of Rome was built in a way that made such an occurrence inevitable. During the reign of Nero, Rome was a busy metropolitan primarily made of crudely constructed shanty towns. The densely packed population of one million lived a daily life filled with fire hazards. On July 18, 64 AD, a fire started at the Circus Maximus, which rapidly broke out through the city and raged for three days. The lack of formal firefighting structures and city planning protocols led to the terrible fire that claimed about 70% of the city.

Nero lost favor with the public in the years following the disaster, even though some records show that the emperor made his palace available to people affected by the flames. Nero constructed an elaborate palace with an intricate colossus of himself, which started the rumor that Nero purposefully burned down the city for selfish reasons. However, there is not much merit to this theory because Nero was miles outside the city when the fire occurred, but nothing else matters besides public opinion in politics. The emperor blamed the persecuted Christians for starting the fire, fueled by his conspiratorial mind. At the time, Rome was divided into 14 districts, of which three were decimated, and only four stood untouched by the huge fire. In addition to the fire, social unrest added to the devastation as looting was widespread during this tumultuous time.

The negative impacts of the fire would never truly escape Rome. The loss of public favor preempted the rise of Julius Caesar and the downfall of Nero, who would die by suicide after 14 years of ruling. The widespread panic and disenfranchisement of the population led to them losing faith in the emperor's power. Furthermore, the fire started a financial crisis and a currency freefall from which Rome would never fully recover. The fire reshaped the economy and political landscape of Rome forever.

This disaster highlights how propaganda can develop from an unsatisfied population. The legend that still lives on in the imaginations of many is how Nero fiddled while Rome burned to ashes. Most historians no longer accept this myth as fact because the emperor was 35 miles away in Antium. Furthermore, the fiddle was not yet invented when Nero ruled, but the leader was known to be an avid lyre player, which is where the legend may have drawn from to construct the shocking story. Other stories are similar to the fiddling legend, with a few accounts outlining that Nero danced on his rooftop, singing the Greek song: "The Sack of Ilium" while the inferno grew to immeasurable proportions. Nero's fiddling has become the symbol of a careless government that feels so little for its citizens that they could party while their city is on the brink of total destruction.

Nero did not do much to repair his reputation after the great fire had left large sections of the population without anywhere to turn. Instead of using Roman funds to help the struggling citizens, Nero selfishly decided to use up the empire's financial resources to construct the decadent Domus Aurea palace complex, which translates to "Golden House." The insane palace included a 100-ft gold statue of the emperor. People in Rome suffered while this ridiculously narcissistic statue towered over them, so there's no wonder why Nero garnered resentment among the broader populace.

Nero's brutality has become legendary in the modern world as many theologians report how gruesome his treatment of the rising Christian movement was. Nero lit Christians on fire as a light feature in his garden parties and would often have them publicly ripped apart by dogs. Nero inadvertently helped spread Christianity because Christian suffering resulted in believers being martyred, which drew many to the faith because they marveled that someone would be so committed to their god that they were willing to die.

The Great Fire of Rome taught future empires many lessons. Firstly, it showed the importance of public opinion so that potential leaders could consider how the masses would receive their actions. The fire also showed the importance of myth as Christian martyrdom grew the religion following their persecution because Nero blamed them for the fire and the popular story of Rome burning as Nero fiddled. On a technological and architectural level, it showed the importance of city planning and having safety protocols in the future, like a dedicated firefighting unit.

The Colosseum: Damages, Repairs, and the Unforeseen Changes Caused by the Hypogeum

The Colosseum is Rome's most iconic structure. The amphitheater creates images of roaring, blood-thirsty crowds cheering as gladiators fought or as a lion ripped a criminal sentenced to death to pieces. For much of Rome's existence, the Colosseum was the center of the empire, where the Emperor's political might was shown and the masses were entertained. Even in the modern era, people flock to the historical site to understand how their ancient human ancestors might have lived. As much as the Colosseum is legendary, it was not always smooth sailing when it came to the construction and maintenance of the building.

The Colosseum.
Sam valadi, CC BY 2.0 <https://creativecommons.org/licenses/by/2.0>, via Wikimedia Commons https://commons.wikimedia.org/wiki/File:Colosseum_-_Rome_-Italy_(16800139540).jpg

After the Great Fire of Rome, Nero constructed his elaborate palace. Now, understanding the importance of public opinion, Emperor Vespasian constructed the Colosseum as a symbolic gesture of giving the palace back to the people. In 80 AD, the Colosseum was completed by the emperor's son, Titus. The magnificent architectural marvel entertained the masses with a range of spectacles. One of the main attractions was Emperor Titus flooding the amphitheater to have a mock naval battle. This battle included prisoners who were meant to be executed. Most of the participants drowned, but those who survived were shown mercy.

The emperor who followed Titus was Domitian. Domitian was responsible for constructing one of the key features of the Colosseum that still stands today: the Hypogeum. This complex underground network of tunnels and trapdoors allowed incredible shows to be put on in the Colosseum, where gladiators, animals, and set props did not have to enter through doors, but they could pop straight out of the ground, creating a shocking and unpredictable atmosphere. Pulley systems that were powered by Judaen enslaved people, who also helped construct the megastructure, allowed platforms to be lowered and raised in an awesome display.

However, with all its benefits, Domitian's mistake was not accounting for how the popular attraction of flooding the amphitheater for mock naval battles would work. The tunnels meant that this marvelous feat could never be recreated. In a culture that valued prestige, pomp, and spectacle as much as the Romans, it was a hit to Domitian's reputation that he could not put on the same show that Titus did. The flooding of the Colosseum was now constrained to the texts of historians, while Domitian would never be able to recreate it.

This blunder was not as huge of a hit as the defeat at Teutoburg or the Great Fire of Rome; it is a smaller pimple on the bigger picture of the empire. The Colosseum is an architectural marvel that remains standing after nearly 2,000 years, even though it has deteriorated and taken a serious beating. The marshy swamp where the Colosseum is located required builders to dig deep foundations, and the construction used concrete. The combination of these two factors is why the iconic structure has stood the test of time. However, the upper levels of the Colosseum did not survive because they were made out of wood. A fire in 217 AD destroyed the wooden sections. Using wood in the structure was a miscalculation, especially considering Rome's devastating past with fires.

The lack of great building techniques, along with bad decisions, has been exposed by the test of time. As Rome Christianized and took the center of the empire east, the Colosseum was neglected and became a dilapidated shell of what it once was. Some see the abandoning of the Colosseum as a cultural center and a marker of Rome starting to fall. The lack of repair and maintenance as the empire transitioned into the Byzantine period was the final blunder that put the nail in the coffin of the Colosseum as a functional venue. The Colosseum has been resurrected as a symbol of modern Italy, and it still holds the attention of masses across the globe.

Rome's expansionism and the narcissism of its emperors seem to be what spelled its doom in the end. Over-ambition and the desire of the elite to stamp their mark on the empire resulted in many terrible decisions. Over time, these blunders compounded, causing the end of the world's most powerful empire.

End of Chapter Questions

1. What were the long-term ramifications of the Battle of the Teutoburg Forest for Rome's territorial ambitions in the northern regions?

2. To what extent have historical accounts and popular culture mythologized Nero's role during the Great Fire of Rome?

3. How did the intricate design and subsequent modifications of the Colosseum's hypogeum impact the events and spectacles hosted within this iconic amphitheater?

Fun Facts

- After the humiliating defeat at the Teutoburg Forest, it's said that Emperor Augustus would anxiously pace the hallways of his palace, yelling, "Quinctilius Varus, give me back my legions!"

- The legendary story of Nero playing a fiddle while Rome burned is not entirely accurate because the instrument had not yet been invented. Nero played the lyre, but historians argue about the authenticity of this account as well.

- M mock naval battles were among the most popular attractions in the early Colloseum. Before the hypogeum was constructed, the entire Coliseum could be flooded for this spectacle.

Chapter 5: Mesopotamian Mistakes

Mesopotamia is the progenitor of all civilization. In many ways, the ancient Metropolitan is the mother of the modern world. So much of what people consider a part of society today has its roots in Mesopotamia. The Sumer people were among the first to develop complex agrarian communities that evolved into cities. Moreover, the Akkadians, under the leadership of Sargon of Akkad, are often mentioned as the first empire, with their political and military success spanning vast regions of the Near East. Written language grew out of the region, with early pictograms later transforming into the cuneiform script. Their innovations in architecture, irrigation, art, culture, religion, and conquest shaped society so intrinsically that it is difficult to picture a world without their contributions.

The creativity and innovation needed to carve out previously unexplored paths require reckless bravery. Stepping into the unknown without a torch or a map can be scary, but the curious and courageous paved the way for society as it is known in the modern age. Sometimes, diving in head first pays off; other times, the consequences are terrible. Most of the time, it is somewhere in between, where taking a step causes other chains of unforeseen circumstances. Through the mistakes of the Mesopotamians, explore how the human spirit can overcome obstacles.

By gazing through the telescope of history, you can unveil how civilizations rise and fall as a result of seemingly small mistakes or miscalculations. Furthermore, watch how greatness can tumble down into nothing from being overly ambitious. There is always an infinite well of lessons that can be unpacked by exploring fallen empires. Examining the first conquerors reveals much about the current human condition and the changes that can be made in real-time to improve the quality of life globally.

Mesopotamia is a fountain of triumphs and failures flowing into the sea that built today's globalized world. As you dive into the blunders of the Sumerians and Akkadians, a mirror is held up to reflect many of the flaws modern people share with their ancient ancestors. Societies continue to collapse and rise along the same lines that were once explored blindly in the past. Although some of the limitations of the past have been transgressed, there is still much to learn. As society changes, many of the failures of the past seem to reemerge. Delving into catastrophic failures in depth can help you understand which ideas, principles, and ideologies are best suited to push society forward on a favorable path.

Ziggurat of Borsippa, or the "Tower of Babel"

There is an undeniable connection between Mesopotamia and the Biblical narrative. Babylon is referred to in the pages of the ancient holy book, and King Nebuchadnezzar II is mentioned by name. Although the Bible is not considered an absolute authority by many, the historical significance of the culture-shaping book cannot be reasonably argued. Nebuchadnezzar II is a prominent character in the account of the prophet Daniel. His role in the destruction of Jerusalem and his defeat of the Egyptian army is recorded in the Biblical Old Testament.

The Tower of Babel.
https://commons.wikimedia.org/wiki/File:Pieter_Bruegel_the_Elder_-_The_Tower_of_Babel_(Vienna)_-_Google_Art_Project_-_edited.jpg

Another Biblical story that Nebuchadnezzar II has been linked to is the Tower of Babel. Genesis 11:1-9 tells the story of when humankind spoke one language. According to the Biblical passages, people gathered to build a tower up to the heavens. However, God was not pleased with this, so He confused their languages, and they could no longer collaborate to achieve their goal. Some parallels can be drawn from this Biblical account to the Ziggurat of Borsippa. Ziggurats are large step pyramids that were built to honor various gods in the ancient Near East. One of the most famous ziggurats in the world is in the historical city of Borsippa.

The ziggurat was constructed by King Nebuchadnezzar II and was dedicated to the god Nabu, the son of Marduk. It gets interesting with Sir Henry Rawlinson's discovery of clay cylinders that date back to 600 BC (Eames, 2018). The inscriptions on the clay tablets may have been commissioned by Nebuchadnezzar II. They outline how he completed the Tower of Borsippa from the abandoned project of a previous king who was building the Tower of Babylon, or as the Bible calls it, The Tower of Babel. Like many conquerors in his time, Nebuchadnezzar II constantly found himself looking for ways to validate his leadership and ensure his name would echo into the future. Unlike the forgotten king who started the project, Nebuchadnezzar II knew that he had to leave a standing monument to his gods for his name to remain relevant throughout the ages.

The inscription of Nebuchadnezzar II describes how the incomplete tower reached 42 cubits before the construction site was abandoned. Therefore, the initial construction of one of the world's most significant ziggurats failed. The goal of the previous king, who had started the construction, may have been to build an incredibly huge ziggurat, but his overly ambitious plans were not realized due to the long build timeline and the water damage the clay brickwork suffered. The tower Nebuchadnezzar II constructed is likely a lot smaller than originally planned to avoid running into the same construction issues of the previous king. This inscription has been used to link the building of the original tower to the epic failure of the Tower of Babel in the Bible.

There are strong connections to the Genesis account. For example, Nebuchadnezzar II explains how the building was abandoned without the people working on it saying anything about it; isn't that odd? There is a correlation between the confusion of languages that the Biblical God facilitated and the fact that they never spoke about why they abandoned the project. The name of the king who started the construction was not mentioned either, but Nebuchadnezzar II outlined that the ziggurat was deserted 42 years before he completed it. Another interesting connection between the Bible and the ziggurat is the name Borsippa, which can be translated to "tongues" or "languages." The story of the Tower of Babel speaks about how all the tongues of the nation were developed when God confused the languages of everyone working on its construction. This strikethrough line that runs across the Bible and Mesopotamia indicates that the ancient civilization may have been instrumental in developing the Abrahamic faiths.

The ziggurat ruins are still standing but have been badly damaged throughout the ages due to war, weather, and looting. Some of the innovations that Nebuchadnezzar II introduced to ensure that the ziggurat would not suffer the same fate it did in the past was the use of intense fire to heat the clay bricks in parts of the building so that they fused and were more resistant to water. These structural changes somewhat paid off because the building at least lasted throughout the reign of the king. Although improvements were made and the project was completed, it was by no means perfect. The bitumen and reed matting used to stabilize and reinforce the structure's core resulted in spontaneous combustion that engulfed much of the holy site. In the 4th century BC, the Persians conquered Borsippa and destroyed many of the temples in the city, including the ziggurat dedicated to Nabu. Eventually, Alexander the Great finished off the city in a plundering that it never recovered from.

The building materials, ambition, and construction timelines were major issues in the ancient world. Today, the ruins offer great historical value and archeological treasure, giving humanity a peak into the world's oldest civilization. The completion of the project by Nebuchadnezzar II, correcting the mistakes of his ancient predecessor, shows how much progress was made in engineering and architecture from the time the civilization first began blossoming until its height. Through trial and error, people learn and improve upon what came before them. In the case of Nebuchadnezzar II, he literally built right on top of the failures of previous generations while still honoring their attempts through heartfelt inscriptions.

Borsippa was a marketplace filled with all kinds of skilled craftspeople. They would not have been able to develop to the high level they were respected for without some mistakes being made. Borsippa teaches the world that building something great takes time and that many obstacles will be overcome. Furthermore, the temple of Nuba was built on top of the foundations of a structure that began decades before, which is a literal and symbolic representation of how society builds on the mistakes of its forerunners. The Biblical bonds further serve to highlight the interconnectedness of various cultures. Babylon may be highlighted as an enemy of God's chosen people in the Biblical narrative, but the Mesopotamian culture undoubtedly shaped much of the Israelite way of life. This again serves to underline another paradox of conflict bringing assimilation and acculturation.

Conquest Kills the Empire: King Sargon of Akkad

Being overly eager is a common theme for the failure of ancient conquerors. As the head of the first empire, Sargon of Akkad invented the trend. Sargon of Akkad had a mythologized life story similar to Moses's in the Bible. The fact that the myth sounds so close to the life story of Israelite lawgivers may be a coincidence, but considering the region and the reality that these cultures interacted, it would not be strange if these motifs were borrowed from one another. The ruler was born to a priestess mother who sent him down a river where he was found and raised by common laborers. Later, Sargon would meet the goddess Ishtar, who lovingly guided him throughout his life. This story was probably crafted as propaganda to justify the King's right to rule. In these ancient societies, there was no democracy, and leadership resulted from a birthright, so crafting a miraculous, mystical story would work wonders for the broader population to accept your rule.

King Sargon of Akkad.
https://commons.wikimedia.org/wiki/File:Sargon_of_Akkad.jpg

Akkadians studied under Sumerians and learned many of their ways. Both the Sumerians and the Akkadians lived in Mesopotamia, so their cultural exchanges were expected. The flourishing Sumerians, who had developed writing, complex mythologies, the oldest zodiac compiled by skilled astronomers, and made agricultural innovations, taught the Akkadians the ins and outs of their civilization, which was rewarded by the Akkadians rising as their rivals. Sargon started his political career as the cupbearer of the king of Kish, which he eventually overthrew. He ruled the city-states of Ur and Uruk, from which he conquered much of Mesopotamia, installing his governors. He defeated Lugalzagesi of Sumer, and an inscription bragging about his 34 decisive battle wins in the Persian Gulf was carved. At its peak, from its central city of Akkad, the Akkadian empire controlled the area consisting of modern central Turkey, Syria, Iraq, and parts of Iran.

Sargon's empire lasted for about two centuries, which is okay for the first empire but is short-lived compared to some other famous conquering nations. Sargon's flaw was that he thought about power, glory, and expansion instead of long-term sustainability. The Akkadian empire abruptly ended – as many parts of the region as possible were abandoned due to changing climates bringing on extreme drought. The cities established under Sargon's rule and inherited by his sons would meet their demise after the invasion of the Gutians. As an empire, being ill-prepared for the changing natural environment will cause its demise. The natural world is just as important, if not more so, than political and military power because your resources grow your economy, and once they are destabilized, *everything else will soon follow.*

Sargon's empire was successful while he was alive due to the favorable conditions under which he conquered. Amazing weather resulted in an agricultural surplus all over Mesopotamia. The favorable climate, abundant resources, and valuable skills allowed Sargon to build up a wealthy and prosperous empire. Furthermore, Sargon plundered the wealth of the lands he conquered, contributing to the growing power of the empire. However, Sargon built an imperial system that was not resilient. Unlike the later Romans, who were able to reinvent the empire continuously for 1,000 years, when hardships hit the Akkadian empire, they crumbled.

Climate change ushered in a drought that destroyed the rich agriculture the empire relied on to maintain itself. This caused many cities to be abandoned as people searched for greener pastures.

Moreover, the resulting unrest and famine caused political instability and infighting that decayed the empire, allowing foreign invaders to take over. The empire eventually dissolved into two sections in the following decades: the Assyrian Empire and the Babylonian Empire, also mentioned in the Biblical narrative. In ancient times, this area of the planet was alive with development, and it continues to capture the imagination of billions worldwide. The more one studies the details of Mesopotamia, the more the actions of civilizations in the modern age make sense, and their growing failures become clearer as well. To prevent present societies from meeting similar ends, it is essential to make the necessary adjustments in order to depart from the destructive blueprint of the past.

Sargon failed to diversify the wealth of his empire, even though he facilitated trade as far as India. Their reliance on agriculture to maintain their civilization was an oversight that Sargon did not have the information to be able to predict. Remember that Sargon was one of the first conquerors, so he did not have much of a blueprint to draw from. Expansionist ambitions require long-term planning and vision. Contingency plans about how to feed the empire in times of droughts and other natural disasters are needed. The relatively quick collapse of the empire proved the difficulty of governing vast lands, especially in times of lack. The disunity of the empire quickly became apparent once the era of milk and honey had ended.

Sumerian Irrigation Poisons the Soil

Sumer was an agrarian culture that made leaps of innovation in agriculture. As one of the first civilizations, the Sumerians' agricultural practices would inspire societies for centuries to come. The ancient Mesopotamians were fighting a few problems as the population grew. People settled in the Zagros Mountains, where it rained regularly. However, the hilly terrain meant that there was little arable land, which became apparent as the population grew. This resulted in many people opting to live in the flat plains along the Tigres and Euphrates rivers. There was space for settlements and crops, and the flat ground was easier to work with than the rugged hills that people inhabited before.

People eventually moved to the Zagros Mountains.

Living on the flat plains meant a lot more land to sustain the population. However, this came with its own set of problems. The plains were dry for most of the year, leaving the land unworkable. Seasonal floods provided the water the farmers needed, but they, too, could be occasionally devastating because the volume of water the floods brought was sometimes overwhelming. This motivated the local Mesopotamians to begin innovating. They built earth walls and levees along the river, with small holes to let some of the water out. In this way, they could control the water flow in their farmlands.

Later, as the population grew, their irrigation methods became more sophisticated. The Sumerians built dams and canals to evenly distribute the water they needed for farming. The irrigation systems became so big that small collectives of farmers could no longer maintain the increasingly complex system. Therefore, governance and organizational structures were introduced to help the farmers work together to maintain the massive project. From these agricultural beginnings, Mesopotamia developed multiple walled cities that would bring forth culture-shifting innovations like writing and develop mythologies that would influence religions for millennia to come.

Although the irrigation systems of Mesopotamia were partly responsible for its growth as the cradle of civilization, their farming practices eventually resulted in its downfall. The groundwater systems of the dams and canals gradually deposited salt into the soil. Over time, the impacts started to become apparent as the farmers had to switch from wheat to barley because it could survive the salinated soil better. About 70% of the land that made up Mesopotamia is salinated (Abdullah et al., 2020). About 4% is severely saline, while 20% is slightly salinated, and 50% is moderately salinated (Abdullah et al., 2020). Therefore, the integrity of the soil was permanently and irreversibly altered.

Eventually, the salinated soil could no longer support enough crops for the local population. Farmers once relied on surplus crops to trade, but now the predominant agricultural products that supported the economy had collapsed. As food security and the economic well-being of the ancient civilization fell, so did their political and military might. The vulnerable society, now unable to support or defend itself, fell to outside forces, spelling the end of the once-powerful Sumerian society.

Although their irrigation systems were far ahead of their time, the Sumerians still had some blind spots. Their water problems were solved, but they did not understand some of the chemical intricacies of the activities they were participating in. Saline soil is acidic, so not many plants can survive in it, so crop output will significantly decrease. The irrigation practices went on for decades, so they made more of their land unfarmable year after year. Again, unforeseen circumstances serve to topple empires. The lessons that can be learned from the Sumer irrigation innovations and blunders and Mesopotamia overall are that extensive research should always be done before taking action and that societies should not craft their economies using a narrow lens.

Like many powerful ancient nations, Mesopotamia's biggest mistakes were caused by a lack of planning and foresight. Mighty rulers do not willingly dive head-first into foolishness; however, success and failure are hidden in the details that are easy to overlook.

End of Chapter Questions

1. How did the design and structural goals of the Ziggurat of Borsippa differ from its actual outcome, and how has it influenced cultural narratives over time?

2. In what ways did King Sargon's efforts to unify and expand his empire contribute to its fragility and eventual fragmentation?

3. Despite their initial success, how did the Sumerians' revolutionary irrigation techniques lead to long-term agricultural challenges?

Fun Facts

- The Tower of Babel is often cited as a Biblical tale, but many cultures developed similar myths. The story ultimately encapsulates the danger of being overly ambitious.

- One of the persevering stories about King Sargon of Akkad, one of history's earliest empire-builders, is that he discovered a baby floating in a basket on the river. The tale shares many similarities with the story of the Biblical patriarch Moses.

- The cuneiform script is one of the oldest forms of writing that evolved from pictographs. The Sumerians developed the script from older iterations, using symbols resembling the communicated concept.

Chapter 6: Chinese Catastrophes

Now, let's head to China for an exciting adventure and witness the grave oversights that marred its illustrious past. You will never guess the backstory behind certain monuments like the Great Wall of China and the blood, sweat, and tears that went into building it. Other interesting stories in Chinese history are so strange you would think they are the plot of a movie. Do you know there was a Chinese emperor who did everything he could to be immortal?

This chapter highlights some of the biggest and strangest blunders in Chinese history.

The Great Wall of China

The Great Wall of China is one of the world's oldest and most impressive monuments. It is over 25 feet tall, spans about 13,000 miles, and took over 2,000 years to finish. Today, it is one of the most significant landmarks in the world, with millions of tourists coming from all over the world to get a glimpse of this ancient masterpiece.

The Great Wall of China.
Photo by CEphoto, Uwe Aranas:
https://commons.wikimedia.org/wiki/File:Badaling_China_Great-Wall-of-China-01.jpg

This wall was built to protect the Chinese Empire from the enemies who wanted to invade and destroy it. However, it was a complete and utter failure that cost the empire more than it was worth.

When you look at the Great Wall, you will probably be amazed by its unique style and massive size. However, you may not know that it was built over the bodies of its construction workers. It is believed that 400,000 men died during the construction of the wall, while others believe the number to be over a million, and they were all buried under the wall. People say that the human remains could fill half the coffins in the country. This is why it is described as one of the biggest cemeteries in the world. It is believed that the bodies were buried either under the wall or near it, but not inside of it, as the decomposed bodies would have compromised its integrity.

This begs the question, why were these people buried under the wall? The government should have given the bodies of the soldiers and the peasants to their families to give them a proper burial, right? Well, the answer to these questions is very disturbing. The remains were used to fill the gaps between the wall and the stones to strengthen the structure. They were also considered a sacrifice to the gods, so they would bless and protect the wall.

Construction on the wall began under the rule of Emperor Qin Shi Huang. He spared no expense to bring his vision to life. Unfortunately, some of those expenses were human lives. The emperor forced convicts, captured enemies, enslaved people, soldiers, and peasants to build the wall. Since all of the Empire's resources went into building the wall, many people struggled to make ends meet. Poverty, famine, and diseases spread among the Chinese people. The workers had to deal with harsh and cruel conditions and were paid very little.

So, was the Great Wall of China worth all these losses?

Before building the wall, the Chinese Empire was constantly threatened by Mongols, Turks, Xiongnu, and others. The Emperors did everything in their power to protect the border, like launching multiple military expeditions and buying off barbarians. However, the attacks didn't stop. They were left with one option: to build a powerful barrier to protect the city. They created a masterpiece and showed the world China's engineering genius, wealth, and architectural expertise. However, this is all it was. The wall wasn't the invincible structure they were hoping it would be. It wasn't impenetrable, and on many occasions, it failed to protect the empire.

Many of their enemies (like Genghis Khan) succeeded in finding the wall's vulnerabilities, enabling them to launch multiple attacks on the city. In 1002, the Tanguts also managed to cross the wall when the guards weren't paying attention. This incident shed light on one of the main weaknesses of the wall: its guards. No matter how strong a defensive fortification is, it can't protect the border by itself.

There were other occasions throughout history that showed how men failed to guard the wall. The biggest blunder in the wall's history took place in 1644 when a Chinese general opened the gates and let in the Manchu forces. The Ming was the ruling Dynasty at the time. They had been fighting the Mongols for two centuries, and they didn't have the strength or the resources to go into another war. The Ming surrendered to the Manchu and put an end to their dynasty, rendering the wall a failure. In fact, in the 19th century, many Chinese people believed the wall was an expensive strategic mistake. Many saw it as a symbol of oppression and death.

No one can deny that the Great Wall of China is a spectacular landmark and a testament to the Chinese people's strength, determination, and capability. However, it will forever be a reminder of all the lives that were lost and its failure to achieve its purpose.

So, was the Great Wall of China worth all the lost money and lives to build it?

Emperor Qin Shi Huang's Obsessive Quest for Immortality

If you had the choice, would you want to live forever? Qin Shi Huang, the mastermind behind the Great Wall of China, was obsessed with immortality. Ironically, this obsession killed him.

Born in 259 BC, Qin Shi Huang was one of the most significant emperors in China's history. His father was the king of Qin, and after his death, Huang took his place at the age of 13. At the time, China was divided into seven cities. Huang was tough, strong, and determined. He unified the country to become one powerful nation and became its first emperor.

Emperor Qin Shi Huang was one of the most significant emperors in China's history.

He managed to achieve so much during this short time as a ruler. He built canals, roads, and the Great Wall of China. Interestingly, he is remembered more for his obsession with immortality than for everything he accomplished.

Qin Shi Huang believed there was a magic potion that could grant him immortality. He even assigned an army of 8,000 men to travel all over the country to find it. Huang believed that his dynasty would last for thousands of years, and he wanted to live to realize his dream.

He sent his men to the Eastern Sea to search for the elixir of life, but they didn't find it. So, he sought the help of the court's magicians and requested they make him a potion that would grant him immortality.

Many people didn't appreciate Huang's obsession, like Confucian scholars who found the emperor's quest to be insane and pretentious.

Huang was more protective over his life than any other ruler. He always had guards protecting him, kept his movements a secret, and built corridors and walls to hide him from the public's eye and protect him from evil spirits.

Huang had a good reason to be obsessed with immortality. He led his army in various conquests, many of which ended in massacres. He was afraid that the spirits of his victims would exact vengeance on him in the afterlife. He also wanted to live forever to realize his dream of a lasting dynasty, so death wasn't an option. Huang went as far as prohibiting any conversation about death in his presence. Many were even terrified to utter the word in front of him.

Huang wasn't the first ruler to be obsessed with immortality. In fact, many of his ancestors shared the same passion. In 400 B.C., there was a rumor floating around that some men found the secret to immortality and liberated themselves from death. Kings were very interested in this story at the time, and many became obsessed with remaining in power forever.

In 320 BC, men taught the art of immortality to kings. When these men died, the kings would be furious for not learning everything from them before they passed. Interestingly, they failed to see that they were being deceived. If these men had the secret to immortality, then why did they die?

One of Huang's ancestors, Qin Shihuang, also chased immortality and believed he would remain in power forever. Like Hunag, he spent his life looking for a potion and believed all the crazy tales his alchemists and magicians told him. Many of them believed that mercury was enchanting. They found the element fascinating and mysterious and even called it the "Elixir of immortality."

In 2002, archeologists discovered ancient documents that showed Huang issued a government decree to every village, demanding they find him the elixir of life. Some of them include correspondence between him and the village's governors. One document revealed that the people of a town called Duxiana looked everywhere for the potion but couldn't find it. Another governor sent him a letter, saying that they found an herb on a mountain in eastern China that was similar to the elixir of life. Clearly, his governors and his people took his request seriously.

These documents reflect Huang's power, leadership, and strength. In ancient times, one should have a strong executive force and a high administration to issue a government decree.

It is believed that Huang consumed a mercury potion, believing it would grant him immortality. They didn't know at the time that mercury was poisonous. Ironically, the potion Huang thought would prolong his life ended at the age of 49. His death led to a civil war, the death of his son, and the collapse of the Qin Dynasty.

Although Huang failed to achieve immortality, he wanted to be prepared and equipped for the afterlife. He knew that he might fail in finding the elixir of life and planned for his death and burial. He built a mausoleum where he would be buried and spend eternity. He also believed he might need an army in the afterlife to protect him from evil spirits, so he had his men build 670 horses, 130 chariots, and 8,000 soldiers out of terracotta. Each terracotta soldier had distinct features, was six feet tall, and weighed about 400 pounds.

Construction began on the mausoleum when Huang was only 14 years old, and his fear and obsession with death started at an early age. Rulers at the time planned their burial during the second year of their reign.

One can't help but wonder if this is a story of a man consumed with power and greed so much that he never wanted to die or of a scared young boy who was holding onto life *because he didn't know what was waiting for him on the other side.*

The Catastrophic Consequences of the Grand Canal

Constructed in the 5th century, the Grand Canal is the longest artificial river in the world, connecting five of China's main water systems. The canal also held tremendous historical significance, connecting the North with the South and strengthening the central governance of the empire. The northern part of the country often suffered from many issues, like drought. The canal delivered food and water supplies to the north from the south, leading to an open communication line between both regions – resulting in cultural exchange. Thanks to this engineering marvel, the economy of all the small towns across the river flourished and prospered. It looks like the canal basically solved all of China's problems, right? In time, the canal managed to defy its purpose and spread famine and drought across the country.

Many things were going against the canal from day one. For instance, its geographical environment was one of the main reasons behind its decline. The government wanted to save resources and manpower, so, during construction, they relied on natural lakes and rivers and artificially dug out sections of the rivers. This impacted the water supply in many areas, and the people were suffering from drought.

The Ming Dynasty had to find a solution to the problem fast. So, they came up with a plan to get the springs from Yuquan Mountain to flow into the Huitong River to increase the water supply. However, this plan backfired. It reduced the water conservancy of the irrigation system – and it failed to solve the drought problem.

The river flowed from the west to the east and intersected with the canal, which spanned from the north to the south. The people expected this to increase the canal's water resources; however, it had the opposite effect. It prevented the rivers from draining to the west, causing instability in the canal. This led to overflow and flooding in different parts of the region, which caused disasters like ships sinking.

The problem persisted, and the water levels were extremely low during the flood season. The increase in water supply was still causing problems in the Grand Canal, Hongze Lake, and Yellow and Huai Rivers.

In the 16th century, they divided the channels of the Yellow River into smaller ones to distribute the water among many regions. However, this plan also didn't work and caused more damage by increasing silting and slowing down the river.

During the Qing Dynasty's rule, the Yellow River's lower parts were clogged. During the flood season, mud from the Yellow River poured into the canal and the Hongze Lake. This silted the Hongze Lake and blocked the shipment port. It seemed that every solution they came up with backfired.

Other factors also contributed to the damage to the Grand Canal. The Ming and the Qing Dynasties made many improvements to the canal. However, they only focused on the transportation aspect and ignored the canal's long-term management planning. For instance, they dug up 430 cubic meters for water supply, which solved the silting problem in the short term. After some time, the water circulation balance was destroyed, which affected the water supply.

The Ming and the Qing only cared about trade and the economy. Their only priority concerning the canal and the Yellow River was water transportation. They ignored the people's needs and livelihood. Their last resort was using the Yellow River to increase the canal's water supply. However, like all their other plans, this one was short-lived and caused huge damage.

All the issues the canal faced were mainly due to politics. During the Yongzheng and Qianlong periods, the government put in a lot of resources so the canal would function properly. This eased transportation in the canal, but only for a short time.

During the Qianlong period, corruption impacted every aspect of the country, including the watercourse administration.

The Qing government invested a lot of money into the canal to guarantee that it operated optimally. However, the administrators working in the watercourse administration were known to steal from this money. They would make up fake expenses and reports, increasing the final cost of a project and putting the rest of the money in their pockets. Since the money didn't go into maintaining the canal, its condition worsened, causing frequent disasters.

This led the government to change the administrators frequently. Not only were they corrupted, but they were also incompetent. All of these factors caused serious damage to the canal.

Eventually, the government focused on sea transport and let the canal be a water supply for the people.

The Great Wall of China has a very sad history that contradicts its grand appearance. It was built on the shoulders of the poor, who gave up their lives to create a fortification to protect their country. However, the wall was a failure, but it succeeded in becoming a famous landmark that brings the country millions of dollars in tourism every year.

The story of Emperor Huang is sadder than it seems. When you have been preparing for your death and burial since childhood, wouldn't you also be obsessed with immortality?

The catastrophe of the Great Canal was the result of poor planning and political corruption. For years, every plan they made to fix problems had the opposite effect. Unfortunately, in all these stories, only the poor paid the price.

End of Chapter Questions

1. While the Great Wall remains an architectural wonder, how did its construction and maintenance expose Chinese strategy and governance vulnerabilities?

2. How did Emperor Qin Shi Huang's fervent pursuit of eternal life ironically hasten his demise, and what implications did it have for the Qin Dynasty?

3. In what ways did the early construction phases of the Grand Canal both enhance and undermine the socioeconomic fabric of ancient China?

Fun Facts

- Despite its fame as a singular structure, the "Great Wall" isn't continuous. It's a collection of walls and fortifications built by various dynasties over centuries, often without interconnectedness.

- The terracotta warriors guarding Emperor Qin Shi Huang's tomb were originally painted in vibrant colors, but most of the paint flaked off within minutes of the statues' excavation due to exposure to the air.

- The Grand Canal, even with its troubled past, remains the longest and oldest canal in the world. Its existence over millennia showcases China's resilience and ability to adapt and innovate through adversities.

Chapter 7: Indian Ineptitudes

When you think of India, what comes to mind? You probably think of the Taj Mahal, yoga, delicious food, and amazing culture. There is no denying that India has a rich and fascinating culture. However, some blunders in the country's history will make you more curious about India.

You will discover in this chapter key failures in ancient Indian history, starting with the mysterious decline of the Indus Valley city of Mohenjo-Daro, the legend of the great King Harsha, and the unfortunate end of Nalanda University.

The Mysterious Decline of the Indus Valley City of Mohenjo-Daro

The Indus Valley (also called the *Harappan Civilization*) was an ancient civilization in north India between c. 7000 and c. 600 BCE. Harappa was one of its largest cities and was the first one archeologists discovered, so they came to refer to it as the Harappan Civilization and its people as the Harappans.

It was one of the most influential ancient cultures in the world, and it can even be compared to Mesopotamia and ancient Egypt. It controlled many regions, like modern-day North India, the Iranian border, and Pakistan. However, it is believed that it might have covered even more countries. One of the most popular cities in the Indus Valley is Mohenjo-Daro, which translates to "Mound of the Dead Men," and it was one of the largest settlements in the civilization.

Mohenjo-Daro was one of the most advanced cities.

Mohenjo-Daro was one of the most advanced cities at the time and was ahead of its time with its urban planning. Although it was built around the Indus River and rain was pretty common in the area, the Harappans didn't only rely on surface water and their climate. They built private and public wells so all people would have water access all year. The largest building in the city was the Great Bath, which included a gentle slope to drain water out of the bath and into a very intricate drainage system.

The drains were placed underground and designed so that they could be easily removed if they required inspecting. All houses had bathrooms with drainage systems. The city also had a developed sewage system, drains to collect rainwater, and large culverts to store any extra water.

Construction in the city took place in a short period of time. They built systems of wells, sewers, and water supplies to support the city's residents. In fact, archeologists found 700 wells in Mohenjo-Daro alone, with bath systems and drainage. Mohenjo-Daro stood out with its interesting architecture and buildings that covered 741 acres.

Indus Valley city was flourishing. It had a population of about 60,000 people and hundreds of settlements. This is why the decline of this rich civilization has always been baffling. In 2,500 BCE, the people started migrating and abandoning their homes. The civilization that once had some of the largest and most developed cities at the time transformed into small villages. In 1,800 BCE, the Indus Valley civilization disappeared, including its two largest settlements, Harappa and Mohenjo-Daro – and even its farming villages were abandoned!

Archeologists discovered that the Indus Valley people used to trade with Mesopotamia, but it stopped with the civilization's decline. The baths and drainage system Mohenjo-Daro was famous for were blocked, and the writing on the wall disappeared.

So, how did the Indus Valley city suddenly decline? What drove the people of a developed and powerful city to abandon it and their civilization? Well, historians have a few theories that can help solve this mystery.

Climate Change

Climate change is one of the most popular theories behind Indus Valley City's decline. The Saraswati River was the city's greatest river and one of its main water supplies. Although small, it was considered a holy river and meant a lot to the people. It is believed that it dried up in 1,900 BCE, leading to climate change. However, other experts believe that there was a huge flood that drove the people to flee for their homes.

Drought, flooding, deforestation, or any other environmental change caused by the river could have caused serious consequences like diseases, starvation, and crop failure. Archeologists also found evidence that suggests many people died from serious diseases, like malaria, which is caused by mosquitoes. Massive loss of life could have impacted the civilization's society and economy.

It is also believed that climate change brought heavy rain, winds, and monsoons. Although monsoons could cause severe destruction, they greatly benefited crop growth. Agriculture was flourishing, leading to the development of its major cities, Harappa and Mohenjo-Daro. The people became dependent on seasonal monsoons instead of irrigation. However, when the climate changed and the monsoons stopped, water sources dried up, and the climate became drier and cooler. Archeologists believe that this led to a tectonic event that changed the river course toward the Ganges Plain. The Indus Valley population might have left their homes and settled in the Ganges Plain, where they built villages and started farming.

Things changed for them after they moved from big cities to live simpler lives in small villages. They weren't able to produce as many crops as they did in Harappa and Mohenjo-Daro, so they couldn't continue trading with big civilizations like Mesopotamia and ancient Egypt. In 1,700 BCE, the impact of all these events led to the decline and collapse of the Indus Valley civilization.

The Aryan Invasion

Another theory suggests that the collapse of the Indus Valley civilization resulted from an invasion. Some scholars believe that there was a European nomadic group called the Aryans who attacked and conquered the Indus Valley city. This theory is based on archeological discoveries where they found unburied bodies in Mohenjo-Daro. They were covered with multiple injuries, leading archeologists to believe that they were victims of war.

The Harappans were peaceful people who didn't care for war. They didn't have weapons or much expertise in fighting. The Aryans, on the other hand, were skilled fighters with an arsenal of advanced weapons and an army of some of the strongest men in the region. They took advantage of the Harappans' peaceful nature and attacked and conquered the city.

However, not all scholars agree with this theory. Some believe that the dead bodies weren't war victims; they were just buried in haste. Others shifted away from the invasion theory. They believe that the city's structural decay drove people out of their homes.

The Indus Valley civilization influenced many ancient cultures. This indicates that it couldn't have just suddenly disappeared. However, scholars still believe that the Aryans were involved. Some think that the Aryans migrated to the Indus Valley, and instead of being influenced by their culture, the Aryans imposed theirs, leading to the decline of the Indus Valley civilization.

The Legend of the Great King Harsha of the Vardhana Dynasty

Emperor Harshavardhana, also called Harsha, was the last ruler of the Vardhana Dynasty... one of the most powerful dynasties in ancient India. He ruled the country for 40 years, and during this time, he achieved military and political success by expanding his kingdom and unifying northern India.

Emperor Harshavardhana was the last ruler of the Vardhana Dynasty.
https://commons.wikimedia.org/wiki/File:King_Harsha_pays_homage_to_Buddha.jpg

Harsha had two older siblings: a brother (Rajya) and a sister (Rajyashri). When their father died, Rajya was supposed to inherit the throne, but he was so consumed with grief that he refused to take it. Harsha had no choice but to become king until his brother returned.

His sister married a powerful man from the Maukhari Dynasty, strengthening the relationship between the two families. The Malwa and Gauda dynasties were the Vardhana's biggest enemies, and they weren't pleased with this union. They attacked and killed Rajyashri's husband and put her in prison.

When Rajya found out what happened to his sister, he took a huge army and went to save her and avenge the death of his brother-in-law. Rajya and his men succeeded in damaging the enemy's army. However, he was betrayed and murdered by the King of Gauda. As a result, Harsha became the official king of the Vardhana Dynasty.

Harsha was no ordinary ruler. He loved his family dearly. When his brother died, he sent his cousin with an army after his killers to avenge him. He also assembled an army and went to rescue Rajyashri. Even though he was a king at the time, he didn't care about his status and only thought about his sister.

At a time when many rulers were cruel and selfish, Harsha was a just king who cared about his people. He imposed fair taxes and gave ¼ of those taxes to charity. However, what set Harsha apart was his love for art and literature. He was a patron of education and put a lot of time, effort, and resources into universities and learning.

In battle, he was a brave warrior who fiercely fought his enemies, and in the privacy of his chambers, he had a more sensitive side, with the pen being his only weapon. Harsha wrote three plays: Priyadarshika, Ratnavali, and Nagananda, which he hired actors to perform before him. Harsha was an author and a poet whose contributions to the literary world were noteworthy. He was highly respected among other authors and even compared to some of the greatest Indian dramatists at the time.

Harsha was a religious man who wrote hymns about Buddhism. He was also responsible for the release of hundreds of poems that honored Buddha.

Harsha seemed like a clever and caring man who did everything right for his family and kingdom. So, what did he do wrong to give him a notable mention in this book?

Harsha was a very ambitious man who wanted to expand his kingdom and gain more power. He fought many battles and was always victorious. His ambition grew with each victory, leading to the Battle of Narmada, where he faced King Pulakeshin II of the Chalukya dynasty. However, Harsha was defeated and forced to retreat with his army. Pulakeshin's victory earned him the title "The great lord or the lord of lords."

Although this was a huge loss, it didn't impact Harsha's army or political power. He ruled for ten whole years until his death in 647 AD. However, the Vardhana Dynasty fell with his demise.

Harsha had two sons, but they were both assassinated. He didn't have an heir to inherit his kingdom after his death. When he passed, his minister, Arjuna, ascended the throne. However, he wasn't as powerful as Harsha, and the empire fell a year later.

The History of the Nalanda University

Founded in the 5th century by Kumaragupta, the emperor of the Gupta Empire, Nalanda University is one of the world's oldest and most influential universities. It is believed that Buddha was a frequent visitor to the university and was quite impressed by it. In the 7th century, Nalanda hosted 10,000 students and 2,000 professors, some considered the best in the world.

The history of Nalanda University is divided into two parts. The first was between the sixth and ninth centuries, and it witnessed its flourishing, growth, and development. The second part was between the 9th and 13th centuries and saw the university's decline.

The university was the home of one of the biggest libraries in the world... the Dharma Gunj Library, meaning "The Mountain of Truth." It contained the biggest collection of Buddhist knowledge at the time.

Nalanda University had a very rich curriculum in every field: foreign philosophy, the scriptures of Buddhism, the Veda, Yoga-shastra, Samkhya, philosophy, metaphysics, logic, medicine, astronomy, and science.

Nalanda was one of the first universities in the world to include dormitories that housed students during the school year. It was also an architectural masterpiece with its magnificent gate and high walls. The university had ten temples and eight compounds, with multiple meditation classrooms, parks, and lakes.

It became one of the most famous universities at the time, attracting students from every part of the world, including Southeast Asia, Sri Lanka, Turkey, Mongolia, Tibet, Persia, Japan, Korea, and China. However, not all students who applied were allowed entry. They had to take a very hard test, and only 20% were accepted. It was considered the center of higher learning until its destruction in 1190.

Nalanda reached its peak under the reign of the Vardhana Dynasty, specifically King Harsha. Since he was highly invested in art and education, he put Nalanda at the top of his priorities. He often donated large sums of money to the university. He also constructed one of its ten temples, which was 100 feet high and covered in brass.

Harsha also donated hundreds of villages to expand the university, allowing it to host thousands of students on its campus. However, he wasn't the only royal to add to the university. Many other kings from different parts of the world contributed to its expansion. Shailendra, King of Indonesia, donated one of the university's buildings.

Nalanda University was one of a kind in every way. Nalanda changed the world with its amazing architecture, interesting curriculum, rare book collection, and brilliant teachers. So, its destruction was one of the biggest losses in history.

In 1193 AD, Muhammad Bakhtiar Khilji, with the Mamluks, Turkish Muslim invaders, attacked India and set the university on fire with its famous library. Since there were millions of books in the library, it took it three months to burn down. They also ransacked the monasteries, and the monks were all afraid for their lives and fled the town.

Khilji wanted to destroy Buddhism, and burning the library that housed their religious teachings was the obvious first step. He saw the Buddhists' immense knowledge and power firsthand and realized they must be stopped. One time, Khilji became very sick. None of his doctors knew what was wrong with him, so he sought the help of Ayurveda, a Buddhist scholar. Ayurveda gave Khilji a medicine that cured him in a short time. Khilji wasn't pleased to see that Buddhist doctors were more knowledgeable than his Muslim doctors. This was one of the reasons that prompted Khilji to destroy Nalanda.

When Khilji burned down Nalanda, he didn't just destroy a university but a part of India's culture, history, and identity. There weren't any universities in India after the destruction of Nalanda for 600 years.

Nalanda's remains became a UNESCO World Heritage Center, attracting tourists from all over the world. It stands as a reminder of what could have been. What would the world have looked like if Khilji hadn't burned it down? The books that were lost will forever be a big scar in history.

Nalanda sank into oblivion for centuries, and everyone forgot about the university – once a beacon for education – until it was re-discovered in 1812. Luckily, Nalanda managed to stand on its feet again and is now opening its doors to thousands of students every year.

Mohenjo-Daro was a modern city stuck in the past. However, its sudden disappearance has bewildered historians for centuries. Was it climate change or the Aryan invasion that put an abrupt end to this ancient city? Whatever the reason, the Indus civilization's disappearance left a fascinating mystery behind that will leave historians intrigued for years to come.

Harsha wasn't your typical ruler. He was a poet and an author who cared about education and charity. Although his empire fell after his death, he will forever be remembered for his contribution to literature.

The destruction of the Nalanda University was a travesty and one of the biggest blunders in history. Not only had India lost a part of its identity but the loss of thousands of books will forever be one of the worst literary tragedies the world has ever witnessed.

The ruins of Nalanda University.
Amannikhilmehta, CC BY-SA 4.0 <https://creativecommons.org/licenses/by-sa/4.0>, via Wikimedia Commons:
https://commons.wikimedia.org/wiki/File:Nalanda_University_ruins_1.jpg

End of Chapter Questions

1. Considering the advanced urban planning and architecture of Mohenjo-Daro, what potential environmental and administrative missteps might have hastened its decline?
2. How was King Harsha different from all other ancient rulers?
3. What lessons can be drawn from Nalanda University's fiery end in the context of preserving knowledge and cultural legacy?

Fun Facts

- The Indus script, prevalent in sites like Mohenjo-Daro, remains undeciphered to this day, making it one of the world's ancient scripts still shrouded in mystery.
- Despite facing multiple military confrontations, King Harsha was also an accomplished playwright. His works give fascinating insight into his time's societal norms and values.
- Nalanda University, established in the 5th century AD, attracted scholars from as far as China, Tibet, and Persia. Its ruins suggest it had a vast campus, including meditation halls, classrooms, and dormitories.
- India has a very fascinating history, with some interesting and mysterious events. One of its biggest mysteries was the decline of the Indus Valley city, one of the most advanced civilizations in the world, which suddenly ceased to exist. Although there are many theories about its disappearance, no one knows for sure what happened. People still wonder about it and ask questions, trying to get a definitive answer.
- Harsha was one of the greatest Indian rulers. When one thinks of kings, one always imagines tough and selfish rulers who only care about themselves. However, Harsha was different. He had a sensitive side and was a writer and a poet. His contribution to the literary world is what makes him memorable. Unfortunately, his death and leaving no heir behind ended his dynasty.
- Nalanda was one of the first universities in the world, but sadly, people only remember it for its sad ending. Stories of its fiery demise and books burning for months are still painful to every knowledge-seeker in the world.

Chapter 8: Mesoamerican Mishaps

The rise and fall of the ancient world of Mesoamerica is a subject of mystery and great interest for many people. By reading this chapter, you'll delve into the mishaps that led to the downfall of what was once an economic, cultural, and architectural epicenter. You'll learn about the ancient Maya of Tikal, why it was an integral Mesoamerican territory, and how a series of droughts and warfare led to its demise. The chapter then delves into Tenochtitlán, the heart of the Aztec Empire, and how a lethal epidemic, along with ruthless schemes, led to its downfall.

The Abandoned Maya City of Tikal

Tikal was an ancient Maya city that served as the largest urban center in the region. It was a significant ceremonial center that was home to a collection of sacred temples and monuments. The city's importance rose drastically from 600 to 900 CE, which was when Maya writing, time-keeping methods, and more pyramids and places emerged. This period was also characterized by the flourishing sculptures, vase paintings, and other forms of art.

Tikal served as the largest urban center in the region.
Shark at the Lithuanian language Wikipedia, CC BY-SA 3.0
<http://creativecommons.org/licenses/by-sa/3.0/>, via Wikimedia Commons:
https://commons.wikimedia.org/wiki/File:Tikalas.jpg

The city also became integral in one of the region's most important trading networks. Tikal continued to thrive even after Teotihuacán, the largest city in the world in 500 CE, declined due to its inability to sustain its growing population. Tikal was at its artistic and architectural height between 600 and 800 CE. However, after suffering a decline in its population, the city followed the fate of Teotihuacán.

Tikal: A Cultural and Architectural Epicenter

The main monuments of the city were organized within one square mile, while other smaller structures, such as homes, spanned the surrounding area, which was over six square miles large. The center of Tikal accommodated around 10,000 people, while the entire population of the city was around 50,000 individuals. Unlike Teotihuacán, which featured closely packed residences and organized streets to accommodate its 200,000 residences, buildings in Tikal were more widely dispersed.

Tikal was characterized by the five pyramid-shaped temples it featured. The city also had three large complexes, which housed palaces and other luxurious structures for the upper and noble classes. A complex includes several buildings, each of which is fortified with a carefully prepared set of burial chambers. As for the pyramids, Pyramid I, which stands at 145 feet tall, is the most popular. The Temple of the Jaguar is found atop the monument. Pyramid II, which is 135 feet tall, is right beside it and crowned by the Temple of the Masks, while Pyramid III stands 180 feet tall. Pyramid IV is the tallest of the five, standing at 213 feet. It carries the Temple of the Two-Heads Serpent, while Pyramid V is 187 feet tall and is found near the Plaza of the Seven Temples.

The Tragic Downfall of Tikal: Droughts and Poisoned Water

Despite being an epicenter of civilization and prosperity for centuries, Tikal was abandoned by the Maya in the 9th century AD. Scholars came up with several theories regarding the downfall of the city. Many suggest that it collapsed for the same reason that the city of Teotihuacán: overpopulation, a lack of sustenance, and the overexploitation of natural resources. Another popular theory was that the area was struck with a period of heavy droughts. New revelations suggest that while the people of Tikal were already suffering from drought, their only drinking water sources were poisoned by toxic substances like mercury and algae.

In efforts to survive the drought caused by the significant slowdown of rainfall for decades on end, Tikal's residents came up with innovative ways to store water. They created large, sloped, and paved plazas that allowed water to slide into the reservoirs. They depended on their reservoirs for survival as the city was closed off from alternative water sources, such as rivers, streams, and lakes. Not only that, but the local water table was low. This meant that the level at which the ground became saturated with water was over 600 feet beneath the ground, which meant that digging wells or attempting to access this water through other means was very challenging.

Researchers studied the sediments of the four reservoirs built in Tikal to better understand all the factors that contributed to the city's downfall. They were surprised to find that two major reservoirs were infested with alarmingly high levels of mercury and extremely dangerous traces of toxic algal blooms.

Everyone knows the ancient Maya were masters of the arts and inventive ideas. However, little did they know that their love for decor and innovation would be the leading cause of their demise. While most ancient civilizations get praised for their lasting contributions to the realm of arts and architecture, the Mayans' iconic red paint led to groundbreaking scientific revelations. While they thought they were adding a pop of color to their surroundings, the Mayans unknowingly added a dash of poison to their diets!

Researchers believe that the mercury found in the pit of the reservoirs came from cinnabar, which is the product of mercury mixed with iron oxide. Cinnabar is a rich red powder popularly used as a pigment and dye at the time. This powder was essential to them because they used it to paint the interiors of the graves of the elite. When examining one of the graves, researchers found around 20 pounds of cinnabar. The excessive use of the powder in and around the temples, palaces, and graves caused a lot of it to wash down the reservoirs whenever there was rainfall. Each drink and meal anyone had was likely laced with mercury.

Their innovativeness didn't stop at the poison-heavy paint. The Mayans insisted on taking things further, creating the world's first algae-themed water reservoir! They didn't realize that what they had intended to be a safe way to store drinking water was actually the ideal environment for the proliferation of blue-green algae because it was rich in phosphate . . . until it was too late, of course.

Phosphate is a nutrient that blue-green algae need to grow. The presence of this nutrient was a product of hundreds of years of cooking fires, smoke, and ceramic dishes washing down the reservoirs. A heap of trash, which the locals threw food waste in, was also kept beside the reservoirs. This meant that plenty of trash slid into the reservoirs during periods of rainfall.

It wasn't until the eruption of algae blooms in the reservoirs that the city's inhabitants guessed something didn't look right. The water in the reservoirs probably looked, smelled, and tasted horrific.

To a highly religious and superstitious civilization, having a poisoned water supply, no access to well water, and years of drought meant that their gods weren't appeased and perhaps mad at the rulers of the city. As the living conditions became tougher to deal with, the locals had no choice but to abandon Tikal and seek refuge in a better city.

The Tragic Downfall of Tikal: Failed Alliances and Warfare

During the same period that Tikal struggled with droughts and undrinkable water, the city went through a series of warfare. The Kaanul dynasty, alternatively known as the *Snake Kingdom*, which ruled from

Calakmul, had a dream of expanding the Maya kingdom to create the greatest one there ever was. Serving as a cultural, economic, and ceremonial center, Tikal was a Maya supreme power that dominated the region's lowlands. The city maintained its position even after Guatemala defeated the Kaanuls. This might've partially been due to the city's alliance with Teotihuacan, which monopolized black and green obsidian trade, manufactured and sent military weapons to Tikal, and controlled Central Mexico. This alliance, however, fell to pieces in the 6th century AD, leaving Tikal in a vulnerable position.

The Kaanul took advantage of Tikal's helplessness, realizing it was a rare opportunity to establish full political control. They wanted to use what was remaining of Tikal's influence to persuade other Maya cities to become allies with the Kaanul. The rulers were especially clever when it came to strategizing methods to build and break alliances between cities, orchestrating ploys that helped them grow their power. They also cleverly got Waka and Caracol to break their alliances with Tikal, further weakening the city's stance. Other major cities that lay on the borders of Tikal, such as Holmul, Saknikte, and Naranjo, also sided with the Snakes. Together, they ransacked Tikal on the 29th of April, 562.

The Downfall of the Aztec Empire

The Aztec Empire was the leading Mesoamerican power during the 15th and 16th century. They controlled one of the largest capital cities in the world, making it at the forefront of politics, economy, and trade. Itzcoatl, the empire's leader at the time, was responsible for creating a coalition between three major Mexican city-states: Tlacopán, Tetzcoco, and Tenochtitlán. While one would expect this Triple Alliance to make the city-states indestructible powers, Tenochtitlán fell under the siege of the Spanish in 1521. This Mexican defeat created leeway for Hernándo Cortés and his conquistadors to overthrow the Aztec Empire.

Tenochtitlán: The Greatest City of All

When Cortés and the Spanish conquistadors, led by Moctezuma II, arrived at Tenochtitlán in 1519, they described it as one of the most beautiful and thriving cities they'd ever encountered. Upon their arrival, the city accommodated around 300,000 residents. It sat atop a manmade island featuring a wide range of picturesque gardens and temples. Even those who resided in different cities were forced to pay tributes to Tenochtitlán's temples and markets. Honoring these holy locations involved making offerings, monetary contributions, and even human sacrifices. These tyrannical regulations resulted in an increasing state of resentment from the other city-states toward Tenochtitlán.

Hernándo Cortés: An Ambitious Spanish Conquistador

Hernando Cortes is a famous conquistador.
https://commons.wikimedia.org/wiki/File:Hern%C3%A1n_Cort%C3%A9s,_Toledo.jpg

Hernán Cortés was the textbook definition of an overachiever. If he wasn't too busy expanding his territory, spreading his faith, and finding enough gold to impress the noblest family of his time, he could've authored a best-selling handbook for conquistadors. Check off all the boxes, and you're guaranteed to bring down an empire!

Hernándo Cortés, one of the most famous conquistadors, settled in Cuba and played a critical role in helping Spain expand its conquests into the Americas. During his stay, Cortés persuaded Velázquez, the country's governor at the time, to permit him to guide a group of conquistadors into Mexico to explore the area. While Velázquez revoked the permission before Cortés could start the expedition, the Spanish conquistador still devised his plan. He was driven by an overpowering desire to expand the Spanish territory, spread Christianity, and exploit the unexplored land's gold, silver, and valuable materials.

Cortés put his own group of eager conquistadors together and led a fleet of 100 sailors and 11 ships, a troop of 508 soldiers, and 16 horses into Mexico on the 18th of February 1519. Upon his arrival on the Yucatán coast, Cortés was immediately told about a group of Europeans who had previously arrived at the area and were immediately captured by the Mayans. He freed Jerónimo de Aguilar, a Franciscan friar who was sent to Panama as a missionary by the Mayans, and Cortés then recruited him. Cortés found that Jerónimo was an incredible addition to his team because he was the only one who knew how to speak the local Maya language, *Chontal.*

Throughout their journey, the conquistadors were gifted 20 enslaved young Maya women. Malinalli, one of these women, was baptized and given the Christian name Marina, and later, she became known as La Malinche. She spoke Náhuatl, the Aztec language, and also the Maya language, Chontal. She was an indispensable asset to Spanish conquistadors because she helped them communicate with indigenous people.

With two people perfecting Chontal on the team, Cortés marched into Tenochtitlán, where they were welcomed by Moctezuma II (alternatively spelled as Montezuma II). The Spanish mastermind, however, quickly noticed that the Emperor's men might turn against his conquistadors and decided to place Moctezuma under house arrest. While he attempted to rule the terrain through the detained emperor's voice, he received news that Velázquez sent men to arrest him for breaking orders. Cortés, therefore, decided to leave Pedro de Alvarado, his left-hand man, to oversee matters in Tenochtitlán as he led a troop to attack the incoming Spanish forces at the coast.

He defeated Velázquez's troops and led the remaining surviving men back to Tenochtitlán. When he came back, Cortés was surprised to find that the lieutenant he had left in charge had killed several hundred indigenous nobles during one of their religious ceremonies, creating a state of disarray among the Aztecs. The inhabitants of the land demanded that the Spanish leave their city alone. Some theorists suggest that the conquistadors murdered Moctezuma as further unrest arose, while others believe that they simply let him die amid a fight.

Garnering Indigenous Allies

After what Tenochtitláns believed to be a successful attempt at driving the Spaniards out of the land, the men soon returned with a small fleet of ships. They were on a mission to get around 200,000 indigenous warriors from Tenochtitlán's neighboring lands on their side. Some of them, such as those from Cempoala and Tlaxcala, had already resented the Aztecs, so allying with them was a fairly easy task. The large army of allies held Tenochtitlán together under siege for 93 days.

After successfully blockading Tenochtitlán, Cortés and his men realized they must stay on their indigenous allies' good side. After all, they were their main source of logistical and operational support. They also used their encampments to launch targeted attacks on the besieged land.

Cortés sent out his fleet in segments to surround the island on which Tenochtitlán is situated, enclosing the land from the water and the causeways that connected it to the mainland. His ships carried cannons that were prepared to launch at any given moment. He also cut off the city's water and food supplies.

To make things worse for the Aztecs, they had to battle a lethal epidemic. Before they departed Spain, some of the highest-ranking conquistadors contracted smallpox. When they arrived in the Americas, they gradually and unknowingly started spreading the virus among the locals. This weakened both the Aztecs they were fighting against and their newly acquired individual allies. Some scholars suggest, however, that the Aztecs were weakened due to the spreading of salmonella rather than smallpox.

The first case of the illness was discovered in Cempola when an enslaved African showed its symptoms. From that moment on, the virus spread exponentially. It reached the Aztecs when the conquistadors and their allies attacked Tenochtitlán together. Nearly all members of the population, from the nobles to the farmers, were affected by the disease, while many Spaniards became immune to it.

The situation grew even worse for the indigenous population as the bodies of those who died from the disease were scattered all over Tenochtitlán. With the city enclosed, the people didn't know how to safely get rid of the bodies. What once was the greatest city Cortés had ever seen had become a large graveyard.

The Decline of the Aztec Empire

During the entire three months that Tenochtitlán was sieged, the Spaniards and their allies launched one attack over the other. Eventually, all forms of Aztec resistance were worn down, and the conquistadors and their indigenous allies marched into the city, turning it into a blood bath. They ruthlessly slaughtered the people and looted and burned down their homes and temples. Cuauhtémoc, the last Aztec Emperor and the son-in-law and nephew of Moctezuma II tried to flee, along with a group of nobles and advisors. The Spaniards, however, caught them and hanged the emperor.

These tragic events led to the collapse of the Aztec empire and dissolved the power of the indigenous people. Three years later, the entirety of Mesoamerica was already under the rule of the Spaniards. They established the colony of "New Spain" and allowed the deadly disease to either kill off or incapacitate what was left of the indigenous population. In addition to being crippled by the life-threatening illness, the indigenous population wasn't nearly as technologically advanced as the Spanish colonizers. While the Spaniards actively used steel and gunpowder against the indigenous people, all the latter had were animal hides, thick cloth, bows, spears, and bladed clubs. Unsurprisingly, they found that the people they sided with to get rid of the merciless Tenochtitlán rule proved to be even crueler.

Reading this chapter invites you to reflect on the exchange of various cultures, intense changes, and, of course, the everlasting legacy that is laced into the history of the Americas. The tales of the indigenous American people are a lasting testament to their endurance and resilience.

End of Chapter Questions

Here are a few questions to reflect on after reading this chapter:

1. How did Tikal's continuous militaristic endeavors, coupled with environmental stressors, play into its eventual abandonment?

2. What strategic and cultural misjudgments made the formidable Aztec capital, Tenochtitlán, susceptible to Spanish conquest?

3. In what ways did Tikal's urban planning, initially a sign of its grandeur, become a factor in its downfall?

Fun Facts

- The ballgame played by the ancient Maya, known as "pok-a-tok," wasn't just a recreational activity. It had deep religious significance, and it's believed that, in some instances, the game ended with human sacrifices.
- Tenochtitlán, built on Lake Texcoco, was an intricate network of canals, pyramids, and causeways, often compared to Venice. When the Spanish conquistadors first saw it, they were astounded by its size and complexity.
- The Pyramid of the Sun in Teotihuacán is one of the largest pyramids in the world. Yet, despite its prominence, the identity of the civilization that built Teotihuacán and its rulers remains largely a mystery.

Chapter 9: Norse Nonsense

All the blunders covered so far have been either in Asia or in America. You are probably wondering if there were any historic mistakes in Europe. Well, there are quite a few. You will travel back in time to Scandinavian countries and discover strange occurrences in their Norse legacy.

The Norse are famous for their fascinating mythology and interesting gods. Who doesn't know about their god of thunder, Thor, and their mischievous god, Loki? You may also be familiar with the lives of the Vikings since they are featured in many TV shows and movies. However, do you know about all the mistakes they made along the way that halted their colonization?

This chapter covers the Vinland Sagas and the Norse ill-fated settlement in North America, the strategic blunders and overreaches of one of their most famous Vikings, and you will learn about their Norse pantheon and the arrival of Christianity.

The Vinland Sagas

Contrary to popular belief, Christopher Columbus wasn't the first to discover America. Other tribes once settled there centuries before he set sail to explore the new world. The Vinland Sagas tell how the Vikings reached these new and unexplored lands. These sagas were written in the Middle Ages and consist of two stories: the Saga of the Greenlanders and the Saga of Eric the Red.

The Saga of the Greenlanders

The story started with a famous Viking, sailor, and merchant called Bjarni Herjolfsson. In 985 AD, he took a trip to visit his parents only to find out they moved to a new land called Greenland. Bjarni decided to sail there and look for them; however, this was an undiscovered territory, and he had no information about it.

While looking for Greenland, the wind blew his ship off course, and he found three lands before him. That was North America. One of them was covered with ice. He landed there and was reunited with his parents. After this journey, Bjarni quit sailing and sold his ship to Norse explorer Leif Erikson, the son of famous explorer Erik the Red. Bjarni was the first European to arrive in North America.

Leif heard about Bjarni's adventures and the new lands he had discovered. Filled with curiosity, he sailed to North America while his father stayed behind. The first land he found was full of forests and mountains, and it came to be called "Helluland," meaning "Stoneland," and the second land was full of forests and hills and was called "Markland," meaning "Woodland." The third one was full of grapes growing in every corner, so they named it "Vinland," meaning "Wineland," and this was where he decided to settle. Some scholars argue that this wasn't how the island got its name. However, the Norse saga mentioned that the island was filled with grapes a few times, so the naming story is most likely accurate.

Many Vikings followed Leif and settled in Vinland. They encountered many natives in the new world and called them "Skraelings," meaning "wretches." Their relationship started off amicable, but this didn't last long. Violent fights often erupted between the Vikings and the Native Americans. As a result, the Vikings only stayed in North America for a short time before returning to their Scandinavian lands.

The Saga of Erik the Red

Icelander explorer Erik the Red discovered Greenland... an island between North America and Iceland. Interestingly, he was the one who gave the icy land its name as a marketing ploy. His son was Leif Erikson, and the story is similar to the Greenland saga with a few more details, except there is no mention of Bjarni.

Erik the Red discovered Greenland.

When Leif's brother, Thorvald, learned of his brother's adventure, he followed in his brother's footsteps and sailed to explore the new world. Upon his arrival to Vinland, he had a huge fight with the natives and killed eight of them. Consumed with vengeance, the natives went after Thorvald and killed him. When their other brother, Thorstein, found out, he decided to sail out and bring his brother's body home. However, he fell off his horse and couldn't reach the boat. He died soon after.

Thorfinn Karlsefni, A popular Icelandic merchant, took his crew and sailed off to Vinland. He was accompanied by two other merchants, Bjarni Grimolfsson and Thorhall Gamlason, who captained their ship.

When Thorfinn arrived, they started trading with the natives. However, the native tribes wanted to trade weapons with the Norse, which Thorfinn was completely against. This led to constant fighting between both sides. Erik's daughter, Freydis, decided to intervene and help her people. She bore her breasts and kept beating her chest with a sword to scare off the natives. Her plan worked, and the natives retreated.

The Norse people stayed in Vinland for three winters. However, constant misunderstandings and fights with natives drove them back home to Iceland.

Norse Settlements in North America

The Vikings had settlements in Greenland's east and west regions, and both supported each other and lived in harmony. The main ones were Helluland, Markland, and Vinland. At first, they could survive by hunting, farming, and fishing. However, this didn't last since there were about 2,500 of them. So, they relied on imported goods.

Reasons Why the Norse Failed in Colonizing North America

Scholars have a few theories on why the Vikings left their American settlements so abruptly. The most common theory suggests that the tense relationship with the natives created a hostile environment for the Vikings. Although the Vikings had better weapons, which gave them a slight advantage during battle, they were heavily outnumbered.

Another theory suggests that Vinland was located far from the other settlements, so they couldn't always get the resources they needed to survive. Greenland also struggled with self-sufficiency and couldn't provide for remote colonies.

In the 14th century, the climate in North America changed drastically, lowering the temperature and making life very hard for the Vikings. They weren't able to sail or hunt for food.

All these factors contributed to the Vikings' short-lived settlement in North America.

Viking Chieftain, Ivar the Boneless

If you watch the TV show Vikings, you are probably familiar with the legendary hero Ragnar Lothbrok. Scholars believe Ivar was Ragnar's son either by blood or adoption, and it is impossible to talk about Ivar without mentioning his equally famous father.

Ragnar married a shaman woman named Aslaug. She told him they must wait three days before consummating the marriage, or their child would be deformed. However, Ragnar didn't listen, and his son was born without any bones, earning him the nickname "Ivar the Boneless."

Scholars can't imagine Ivar's exact condition. Some believe that he was either truly boneless or else he only had no bones in his legs. For this reason, Ivar couldn't walk alone and was often carried on a shield or a stretcher. However, if Ivar didn't have any bones, he wouldn't have survived, so clearly, these records were exaggerated. Modern scholars believe that he suffered from osteogenesis imperfecta, a condition that left his bones weak and fragile. However, other scholars believe he was given this nickname because he was childless and had never been with women.

He accompanied his father and brothers in multiple raids and inherited many of his father's heroic qualities. Ivar was a clever, strategic planner who often led his brothers on their adventures. He had three younger brothers: Sigurd Snake-in-the-Eye, Hvitserk, and Bjorn Ironside.

He was described in ancient Norse documents as a very wise and handsome young man with a very strong physique. It is said that he was nine feet tall, making him one of the tallest people to ever live. He was a very talented archer with unmatched upper-body strength. In battle, he would always shout words of encouragement to his warriors. His voice was louder than an ordinary man's, and all the soldiers in battle could hear him as if he were standing next to them. In fact, he was the main reason why Ragnar was able to achieve victory on multiple occasions.

Ivar, like his father, was a legend. However, he was very ambitious and wanted to be as famous as him, which led to some strategic blunders and overreaches that cost him dearly.

Ivar and his brothers often went against their father's will and ventured into territories he warned them against. In one story, Ragnar appointed Eystein Beli as the king of Sweden and commanded him to protect the realm from his rogue sons. Ragnar also wanted to remain more powerful than his boys and feared they would overshadow him. Eirek and Agnar (Ivar's half-brothers) tried to take over the kingdom but failed and were killed. That drove Ivar, Aslaug, and the rest of his brothers to seek vengeance. After a vicious battle, Eystein was killed, and the boys avenged their brothers.

Ragnar wasn't pleased that his sons achieved a huge victory without his help. He decided to conquer England without them to show them he was the stronger and better warrior. However, Ragnar overestimated his strength. His army was terribly defeated, and he was executed. When his sons learned of their father's fate, they swore vengeance. Ivar wanted to know in detail how his father died so he could be consumed with more anger and hatred.

They gathered a large army and sailed to England. The boys were prepared for war and were willing to fight to the death. However, Ivar had other plans. He refused to fight, and as a result, his brothers faced a terrible defeat and were forced to retreat and return home.

Ivar didn't return with his brothers. He went to the king and told him that he refused to participate in the battle to show his goodwill to him. The king was impressed with Ivar and compensated him for his father's death. He gave Ivar large lands, founded the city of York, and established close connections with the locals.

However, all of this was part of a bigger plan. Ivar was extremely cunning, but he was also loyal to his brothers. He would never betray them. After he settled, he invited them to join him in York so they could try to avenge their father again. This time, Ivar was prepared. He managed to deceive the king into thinking he was on his side, and he had made many new friends. They defeated the king and his army and avenged their father.

Ivar didn't return home after his victory. He remained in England and began his reign of tyranny there. No one was safe from him. The British saw him as a demon from hell since he was cruel and ruthless, and his attacks were brutal.

In battle, Ivar often showed up with half his army to give his enemies the illusion that he was outnumbered. However, the second half of his men would often attack the enemy from behind, securing an early victory.

No one knew exactly how Ivar died. Some say he died suffering from a terrible illness, while others believe that he died peacefully in Ireland. However, it was clear that he didn't die in battle. It is believed that he was between 35 and 45 years old when he passed.

Norse Pantheon and the Rise of Christianity

The Norse pantheon consisted of a variety of gods and goddesses, each with a special dominion and power. They were given human qualities with strengths and weaknesses. Some of them were overly ambitious, greedy, or prone to anger. There were about 66 Norse deities, but 13 of them were extremely significant to the culture and highly venerated.

Odin is the chief of all deities.

- **Odin:** Chief of all deities.
- **Thor:** God of thunder.
- **Frigg:** Goddess of fertility and motherhood.
- **Loki:** God of mischief.
- **Freya:** Goddess of love.
- **Heimdall:** Guardian of the gods.
- **Baldur:** God of wisdom.

- **Freyr:** God of prosperity and peace.
- **Idun:** Goddess of youth.
- **Hel:** Goddess of the underworld.
- **Njord:** God of weather and wind.
- **Tyr:** God of war.
- **Nerthus:** Goddess of peace and prosperity.

The Vikings were devoted to their faith and their deities. They often performed various rituals to appease their gods, like blōt, meaning sacrifice. They sacrificed animals, like horses and pigs, and held feasts for their communities. They took their religion everywhere they went. Whether invading England or trading with other parts of Europe, they held onto their pagan beliefs.

Christians in other parts of Europe saw the Vikings as brutal and uncivilized. You can imagine how the English people felt about the Vikings and pagans during Ivar's raids.

The Vikings were introduced to Christianity in their expedition in Europe. Some were curious about this new faith, while many others remained true to their pagan beliefs. Hákon Haraldsson, the king of Norway, was the first Viking king to adopt Christianity. He tried to convince his people to convert as well, but he was met with opposition. They took to the streets to express their anger by burning churches and killing priests. Some even wanted to sacrifice the king to the gods.

The Norse pagans weren't pleased to see huge numbers of people embracing Christianity, and many tried to reconvert them. This led to even more clashes and tensions between both sides.

So, what attracted the Norse pagans to Christianity? Some were forced to convert as a result of religious and political pressure from countries like Germany. Some Vikings wanted to keep trading with the Christians in Europe, so they converted to their religion. There were also people who found comfort in Christianity – a religion that calls for loving one's neighbor and helping those in need, unlike Norse paganism, which focused on brutal rituals and sacrifices that began alienating its people.

When Christians wanted forgiveness, they went to church and spoke to a priest, but pagans would go to temples and present a sacrifice. Some people started to feel that these practices were outdated. One could also argue that the misinterpretation of certain rituals and sacrifices contributed to the spread of Christianity. Some found their rituals strange or primitive, but they never tried to look at the intention behind them. For instance, women would make offerings to Frigg because she is the goddess of fertility, and they wanted to get pregnant. Even though Christians didn't get the concept of offering or might have frowned upon certain sacrifices, they didn't understand that this was the only type of worship the Vikings knew.

However, the Vikings didn't accept Christianity right away. They were extremely devoted to their gods, and it took centuries to convert most of them.

The Vinland sagas cleared the misconception that Christopher Columbus was the first person to discover America. The Vikings took this journey 500 years before him and managed to live there, build settlements, and have a life that lasted for a few years. One can't help but wonder what the world would have looked like if the Norse people never left and Columbus never set foot in the new world.

Although Ivar is one of the most popular Vikings, his memory is quite tarnished. There is no denying that he was a brave and powerful warrior, but his bloodlust and blind ambition turned him into a killing machine... a man with no mercy.

The Vikings were extremely devoted to their religion and didn't accept Christianity immediately. However, different factors drove them to accept this new religion and let go of their primitive rituals and sacrifices.

End of Chapter Questions

1. What challenges did the Vikings face in Vinland that made it a short-lived venture, and how might different strategies or preparations have changed the outcome?

2. How did Ivar the Boneless's ambitious campaigns, both successful and flawed, shape the trajectory of Viking expansion and influence?

3. In what ways did the gradual shift from Norse paganism to Christianity affect the Viking societies and their interactions with neighboring regions?

Fun Facts

- The name "Ivar the Boneless" is quite enigmatic, with theories ranging from his physical condition to the term being a metaphorical description of his unpredictable nature.

- The Vikings had a rich and varied diet that included foods like pickled herring, dried fruits, and even a type of yogurt called skyr. This diet played a part in their ability to travel long distances and conquer various lands.

- Contrary to popular belief, the iconic horned helmets often associated with Vikings are largely a myth. Archeological evidence suggests that Viking helmets were typically horn-free and were designed for practicality in battle.

Chapter 10: Persian Puzzlements

With a peek into the intricacies of the Persian Empire, this chapter brings you to the end of your journey through the mishaps that shaped civilization. The first story showcases King Darius's incredibly ambitious yet erroneous military campaign against the Scythians, which left his army with a futile chase after the enemy and, ultimately, depleted of resources. The subsequent story shifts to the Battle of Marathon, where another strategic mistake turned a secure Persian victory against Athens into a celebration for the enemy. Concluding the voyage, the final narrative examines the rise and fall of the palace of Persepolis, how Alexander the Great was persuaded to destroy it, and how the failure of Persian defense made this possible.

King Darius's Campaign Against the Scythians

After being confronted with the same problem as many other Eurasian leaders before and after him – the threat of the nomadic people – in 513 B.C., King Darius I of Persia launched one of the most renowned military campaigns of the ancient world's history.

King Darius I launched one of the most renowned military campaigns.

At the time, the biggest threat perceived by the Persians (as well as the Greeks) came from the Scythians, and for this, they became the target of Darius. The Scythians ruled the territory between the Black Sea and the Don and Danube Rivers. Some records suggest that the true reasons behind Darius Scythians' campaign lie in his thirst for vengeance for the decades-long Scytian rule in the region. Supporters of this theory claim that as great and prosperous as the Persian Empire was, Darius was still afraid of the Scythians and couldn't rest until they completely diminished their power. Others argue that ever since the Scythians appeared in Assyria in the 8th century B.C., they caused many losses for the Assyrian Empire, and defeating them would have resolved an issue of historical proportions.

Darius's strategy incorporated unlimited resources and manpower, making the Scythian Crusade one of the most well-prepared military campaigns in history. Due to all the economic and political power in Persian possession, the king had no trouble founding and supporting this campaign. According to the narrative of the Greek geographer and historian Herodotus, the Scythians had a serious advantage when it came to mobility. They knew the terrain and were even able to establish small settlements and sustain themselves by plowing the land despite not staying in one place for a prolonged period and employing the scorched earth tactic. For the same reason, they managed to escape the Persian fleet many times because while the Scythians never stayed in one place for too long, the Persians did, and the Scythians used this to their advantage. However, after chasing them onto the territory that now belongs to Russia, Ukraine, and the Balkan countries, the Persians greatly damaged the Scythian supplies. After using the great rivers in the regions to supply additional reinforcement to their army, the Persians also cut the Scythians from their allies.

Instead of advancing further, Darius consolidated his bounty and built a solid defense line. Moreover, in a move of tactical genius, he didn't attack from the front for a good reason. The part of Scythia farther away from the direct line of conflict between the two troops was far more prosperous. It also consisted of permanent settlements, so conquering it first to gain more resources and a tactical advantage made sense. Translocating his fleet of 720,000 men, bolstered by the Persian navy around the Black Sea and toward the European side of Eurasia, Darius prepared to attack the Scythians from the rear. The trip involved crossing several rivers, so Darius employed Greek engineers to construct bridges. According to Herodotus, Darius's ability to move this massive fleet around speaks volumes both about the precise organization and the immense amount of resources of the Persian Empire during Darius' rule. The incredibly efficient ancient Persian postal system played a massive role in making this possible.

The Persians set up bases in several Greek cities, forcing the Scythians to withdraw from them. From these bases, Darius's army fanned out into Scythian lands, advancing north toward the city of

Gelonnos and the Don River on the fan's southern side. While now respecting the power of the Persian forces, the Scythians continued to pursue their scorched earth policy, attempting to destroy everything in their wake and leaving nothing behind for the Persians to seize. The Scythians sent everyone who couldn't fight away, along with the livestock their army could spare.

At this point, the Persians had already built their fortified line in the north and cornered the Scythians into a barren land that couldn't sustain them. Darius built another line there to prevent them from escaping toward the south. In an incredible maneuver, the Scythians managed to escape on the northern side, forcing Darius to chase them toward the north, and then they circled back to their homeland. Although his plan to starve the Scythians had failed due to their vast knowledge of the territory, Darius hadn't given up. As soon as the Scythians appeared in their homeland again, he ordered the Persian fleet to reverse its course and march back to Scythia as well. Realizing that the Persians planned to move north in order to prevent them from gaining shelter in the thick forest area and forcing them into the territory where they would be trapped between the Persian troops and the Persian land, the Scythians flew until the Baltic Sea. The Persians chased them almost there but returned to their bases near the original Scythian territory. Soon, the Scythians circled back once again and returned to their homeland the second time. Darius' army was worn out from all the chasing and moving around, which encouraged the Scythians. For the first time since the beginning of the campaign, they launched an offensive. Unfortunately, instead of attacking with full force, the Scythians only sent a few troops to execute the attack from the front, while the rest were charged with harassing the enemy's troops from the other side and attempting to persuade the Persians' Greek allies (including the engineers who built their bridges) into betraying them. However, the Greeks refused to budge, and while initially pretending to wait until they could see how the situation unfolded (mainly to stall and avoid direct confrontation with the Scythians), they never betrayed the Persians. Still, by moving close to the bridges guarded by the Greeks, the Scythians put further pressure on Darius' already strained troops. Fortunately, the king ordered them to retreat, after which the Greeks dismantled the bridges at strategic places, which forced the Scythians to return to the land they had previously destroyed themselves.

After three years of chasing, the Scythian campaign came to an end when Darius realized that he would not be able to engage the Scythians in battle or obtain any territorial gains. Therefore, he decided to march back to the previously secured Persian territories.

The Battle of Marathon

While the Greeks didn't confront the Persians during or after the Scythian debacle, they weren't satisfied with how things turned out either. Their dissatisfaction with the Persian dominance in the region grew, and Darius wasn't happy about this either. The Greeks openly supported some of the revolts against the Persians in Iona, causing major headaches to the Persian Empire. At the same time, Darius wanted more power in Europe, and now that his plan to overtake Scythia had failed, he was forced to readjust. His new plan involved closing in on the Greek capital, conquering it, and establishing his dominance in Europe as well as in Asia. This strategy led to the Battle of Marathon in 490 B.C., which occurred in northeastern Attica and marked the beginning of the Greco-Persian War.

While there are few records of the event, Herodotus wrote an extensive account of the battle, albeit these were created half a century later, so some find their accuracy highly questionable. Robert Browning also created a rendition of the battle, although his only goal was to highlight the messengers' run from the battlefield to Athens.

As the Persian army was advancing fast, the Greeks were forced to assemble their troops in haste. These men were led by the Athenian general Miltiades, an excellent strategist and one of Greece's most accomplished military leaders. The two arms met north from Athens, at the plain of Marathon, in September of 490 B.C. Soon, the first battle on the mainland took place. The Persian numbers were reportedly less than 30,000 and were led by Artaphernes, Datis, and Hippias. By contrast, the Athenians had less than 10,000 men, most of whom were rebels who were always ready and available to fight against the Persians. The only Greek allies that joined them were the Plataeans. The rest remained neutral while secretly hoping for Persian victory, as this would extinguish the democracy the Greeks insisted on cultivating.

The Persians had sent the cavalry ahead during the night, and as soon as the sun rose, they were ready to send the infantry as well. Upon hearing of the Persian cavalry being on its way, Miltiades saw that this was the best moment to strike.

Despite the last-minute preparation and the lack of support from neighboring nations, Miltiades was able to deliver a quick blow to the center of Darius's army. This was achieved through a strategic move of spreading outward from the Greek fleet's middle while bolstering the wings. Still, the center was made of heavily armed and seasoned foot soldiers who could hold up against a small-scale attack. The wings were tasked with breaking through the Persian infantry, which, while higher in numbers, had fewer weapons. While the Greek army's center was somewhat damaged, it held on long enough to fulfill its purpose and enable the other troops to break through and get behind the invader army.

This surprised the Persians as their enemy was clearly outnumbered, and they considered the attack a given victory. While they knew that after the cavalry's withdrawal, their flanks would be exposed to a Greek attack, they thought that if this happened, they would either win the fight or, in the worst-case scenario, simply embark their infantry back on the ships and sail off before Miltiades' army reached the edge of the plains. They aligned their ships in a way that would allow a quick retreat, and they calculated that the Greek formation would take at least 15 minutes to advance into striking distance. Unfortunately, their calculations were faulty, and the enemy reached them much sooner. While they were able to embark some of the men, this was only after they were forced to engage in battle with the Athenians who were maniacally running towards them.

Confused, the Persians began to panic, and with their organization lost, so was the battle. Even the Persian Immortals, the group of highly-trained soldiers whose flanks were assembled during the reign of Cyrus the Great (the second king of the Persian Empire), couldn't withstand the surprise attack. Trained since the age of 20 and never older than 50, the Immortals were armed with a small armory, including lances, swords, slings with pellets or stones, maces, battle axes, javelins, two bowstrings, along with composite bows, and a quiver of 30 arrows. Still, they were defeated because they underestimated their enemy. Moreover, they were trapped on the shores and had nowhere to retreat.

Ultimately, Miltiades's genius tactical move earned the Greeks the victory at the Battle of Marathon. According to the tales, the Greek army was so delighted by their ability to defeat the Persians that they immediately sent a messenger to Athens to deliver the news. The messenger ran 25 miles from the plain of Marathon – a journey that ultimately led to the creation of the modern sport of marathon running.

Years later, the Greeks survived another invasion from the Persians at the Battle of Thermopylae (this time, led by Xerxes I, Darius's son) and held it off for several days before King Leonidas of Sparta was forced to surrender. However, the Greeks' magnificent victory at the Battle of Marathon would cement their fame and enter them into history. The winners were dubbed the "Marathon men" and celebrated publicly, and the dead (there were only 192 lives lost among the Athenians and Plataeans, whereas the Persians lost over 600 men) were laid to rest in magnificent burial mounds on the battlefield plain. They were further honored by panoramic murals and epigrams, which were composed a short time later.

The Palace of Persepolis – From Paradise to Destruction

The Palace of Persepolis was a focal point in this majestic city built by Xerxes I, the son and successor of King Darius I of Persia. While Darius himself made plans for building Persepolis as the new Persian capital, most of the work (including the building of the palace) was done during Xerxes's lifetime. Xerxes's son, Artaxerxes I, completed the work a century after his grandfather began it. The palace was preceded by the Hall of Hundred Columns, where the king received guests and military leaders. Officially known as the Kings and Queens Palace, the residence had separate quarters for the king and queen, and the king's relatives and ladies-in-waiting were assigned to every female household member. The palace also had a massive 108,000-square-foot treasury, where the financial transactions (including the hours worked by everyone at the palace and their wages) were recorded on clay and stone tablets. The surviving records show that both sexes were paid equally for identical work, and everyone who worked at the palace enjoyed a comfortable life due to their fair wages.

The Palace of Persepolis was a focal point of the majestic city built by Xerxes I.
Carole Raddato, CC BY-SA 2.0 <https://creativecommons.org/licenses/by-sa/2.0>, via Wikimedia Commons:
https://commons.wikimedia.org/wiki/File:Palace_of_Darius_(Tachara),_Persepolis.jpg

Construction features of the Palace of Persepolis included wood columns (Indian teak and Lebanese cedar were all the rage at the time), which were set on and topped off with stone elements. The latter was built by stonemasons from Sardes and Ionia, while some of the decorations were sculpted by Telephanes of Phokis. The tops were known as capitals and were akin to bullheads supporting the massive wood cross beams set across the "saddle" between them. The cross beams were placed with another two wood beams for support and were bolstered by a matt and thick earth layer. Besides covering and reinforcing the beams, the earthy layer also helped form an adequate ceiling to shield from the elements. However, the ceiling was also finished with a bright, luminous layer of paint to make it more appealing.

Unfortunately, just as it caught the eyes of the many visitors and allies, the city of Persepolis, along with its beautiful palace, also drew the attention of Alexander the Great of Macedonia, who set out to destroy it. According to the account of Diodorus Siculus, Alexander initially only ordered his troops to demolish the city of "their worst enemies" but keep the palace intact.

Given that Persepolis was considered a veritable paradise, the Macedonians readily rushed to plunder and pillage this wealthy city, killing the men and taking their treasures, and the women became slaves.

They found silver, gold, and exquisite dresses in colors made from expensive materials, along with many other riches from all around the world. As great was the prosperity of Persepolis, so was its destruction. Still, as many prizes they'd already won, the royal palace was intact, but not for long because the Macedonians couldn't satisfy their greed.

Alexander himself took possession of the palace, including the treasury. Here, he found riches accumulated since the foundation of the Persian Kingdom, amassed by the first king, Cyrus. Thinking the newfound bounty could repay all the expenses he had incurred during the war, Alexander decided to take as much of it away as he could. According to the records, he hired 3,000 to 5,000 camels and 20,000 mules to carry the Persian treasure to different destinations – some to Susa, some to be distributed among his troops.

Alexander celebrated his grand victory over Persepolis by organizing games and offering sacrifices to the deities he considered his allies in battles. During a celebration in honor of the god Dionysus, as Alexander was feasting with his friends and companions, one of his female guests proclaimed that Alexander's victory wouldn't be complete without destroying the greatest pride of the Persians – the royal palace of Persepolis. She proposed that the Macedonian women, accompanied by Alexander himself, form a procession and set the palace on fire. In their drunken stupor, the men were excited by this idea and immediately rose to the challenge, lighting torches and shouting their intent to finally punish the Persians for all the damage they did to the Greek religious cities during the conquests. Still, some consider that it should be Alexander who set the palace ablaze, encouraging him to join them as they formed the procession that would lead them to the palace. Alexander took one of the numerous lit torches and started to lead the Macedonians, who accompanied him by singing and playing cheerful songs on flutes and pipes. He was the first to throw his blazing torch onto one of the wooden elements of the palace, after which the men and women from the procession followed suit. Surrounded by glowing torches, the entire monument was soon engulfed in flames, Alexander's triumphs were complete, and one of the grandest royal palaces from the ancient world ceased to exist.

The story of King Darius' war campaign against the Scythians is a prime example of how one man's ego can drive them to showcase their power in nonsensical acts, like sending an army on a wild-goose chase after the enemy on unfamiliar territory.

Likewise, in the third story, despite his initial determination to capture and keep the Palace of Persepolis to himself, Alexander the Great was persuaded to destroy it in an attempt to declare his might.

The story of the Battle of Marathon is simply a case of a baffling miscalculation that had great costs for the Persians.

End of Chapter Questions

1. What tactics employed by the Scythians during King Darius's campaign rendered the formidable Persian military machine ineffective?

2. In the context of the Battle of Marathon, how did Persian military strategy, often seen as invincible, falter against the Athenians?

3. How did the architectural grandeur and cultural significance of Persepolis become a vulnerability during the onslaught of Alexander the Great?

Fun Facts

- The Persian postal system, famously remarked upon by Herodotus, was the epitome of efficiency. Their ancient saying was: "Neither snow, nor rain, nor heat, nor gloom of night stays these couriers from the swift completion of their appointed rounds," a sentiment later adopted by the U.S. Postal Service.

- The name of the Persian Immortals, an elite fighting force, originates from the practice that allowed that if any member was killed or wounded, they would be immediately replaced, ensuring their fleet counted exactly 10,000 at all times.

- The Persian Empire introduced the concept of "paradise" as an enclosed garden. The term "paradise" hails from the Old Persian word "pairidaeza," which means "enclosed space."

Conclusion

As powerful civilizations rise and fall, the lessons they leave society with and how they restructure the world impact people's lives for centuries to come. From imperial expansionist attitudes stretching the resources of empires too thin to the mismanagement of resources and a misunderstanding of nature, human curiosity uplifts society, but it also causes it to fall. The limitations of the human mind and the undiscovered truths of existence lead people to make decisions without fully understanding reality.

People are hardwired to seek out constant progress in order to gather more resources, make life more comfortable, and increase their overall well-being. Progression requires journeying into the unknown, so when revolutionary minds push for change, there is always a chance of failure. Moreover, the pursuit of making life palatable through hardships makes people grab hold of new technologies without fully understanding the outcomes. Humanity seems to be stuck in a similar cycle, even in the contemporary world. People are flawed, so their actions will embody their shortcomings, prejudices, and cultural programming.

As the world has become increasingly interconnected and globalization is the order of the day, the hasty decisions that a few elite groups make and the bigger societal practices the masses embrace will be far more impactful than in past civilizations. Couple that with the rapid development of technology that most people hardly understand, and it seems like humanity is on the fast track to several more big blunders and mess-ups of epic proportions.

However, the past has shown that humans are resilient. The constant failures at every step of human development contributed to a well of knowledge that allowed others to overcome obstacles that once destroyed entire cultures. In this cycle of failure and growth, it is nearly impossible to tell what position you are holding. The road to prosperity and destruction can be indistinguishable at times, only becoming clear when you are near the journey's end.

The complete story of human failure has not yet been told as long as people still inhabit the planet. Maybe with space exploration, people will be allowed to fail **upward** on other worlds. As individuals look into the past and analyze epic failures, society can see how it has grown and, disappointingly, how it has stayed the same. The project to make life better for all while actualizing your identity is still ongoing, and nobody knows how it will end. The beautiful part about it all is that although the journey can either be great or terrible, there is no doubt that it will not be boring.

If you enjoyed this book, a review on Amazon would be greatly appreciated because it would mean a lot to hear from you.

To leave a review:
1. Open your camera app.
2. Point your mobile device at the QR code.
3. The review page will appear in your web browser.

Thanks for your support!

Check out another book in the series

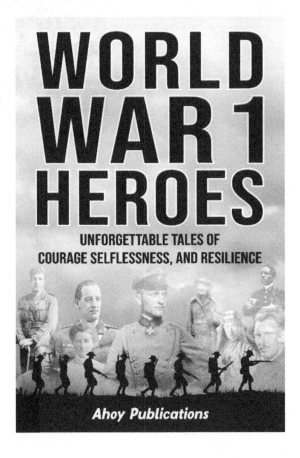

Welcome Aboard, Check Out This Limited-Time Free Bonus!

Ahoy, reader! Welcome to the Ahoy Publications family, and thanks for snagging a copy of this book! Since you've chosen to join us on this journey, we'd like to offer you something special.

Check out the link below for a FREE e-book filled with delightful facts about American History.

But that's not all - you'll also have access to our exclusive email list with even more free e-books and insider knowledge. Well, what are ye waiting for? Click the link below to join and set sail toward exciting adventures in American History.

Access your bonus here!

https://ahoypublications.com/

Or, Scan the QR Code!

Thanks for your support!

References

24 Facts about The Colosseum. (2021). The Colosseum. https://www.thecolosseum.org/facts/

Alatalo, E. (2015, November 30). 4500-Year-Old Urban Planning at Mohenjo-daro. Field Study of the World. https://www.fieldstudyoftheworld.com/4500-year-old-urban-planning-at-mohenjo-daro/

Anand. (2015, January 13). Harshavardhan's Empire: Sources, Accession and Other Details. History Discussion . https://www.historydiscussion.net/biography/harshavardhans-empire-sources-accession-and-other-details/3084

Barrett, A. (2020). Rome Is Burning: Nero and the Fire That Ended a Dynasty. Princeton University Press.

BBC News. (2017, December 25). How China's First Emperor Searched for Elixir of Life. BBC News. https://www.bbc.com/news/world-asia-china-42477083

Boey, J. (2022, November 4). The Human Cost of the Great Wall of China. Dr. Justin Boey. https://justinboey.com/the-human-cost-of-the-great-wall-of-china/#google_vignette

Bordewich, F. M. (2006, September). The Ambush That Changed History. Smithsonian Magazine; Smithsonian.com. https://www.smithsonianmag.com/history/the-ambush-that-changed-history-72636736/

Bressan, D. (2019, October 30). Climate Change Caused the World's First Empire to Collapse. Forbes. https://www.forbes.com/sites/davidbressan/2019/10/30/climate-change-caused-the-worlds-first-empire-to-collapse/?sh=750d912044e1

Brinkhof, T. (2023, September 26). Herostratus: The Man Who Destroyed an Ancient Wonder of the World. Big Think. https://bigthink.com/the-past/temple-artemis-herostratus-destroyed-ancient-world-wonder/

Callaway, E. (2024). The Discovery of Homo Floresiensis: Tales of the Hobbit. Nature, 514(7523), 422–426. https://doi.org/10.1038/514422a

Carrillo, K. J. (2021, May 20). How Hernán Cortés Conquered the Aztec Empire. HISTORY; History.com. https://www.history.com/news/hernan-cortes-conquered-aztec-empire

Cavendish, R. (2015, September 9). Discovery of the Lascaux Cave Paintings. History Today. https://www.historytoday.com/archive/months-past/discovery-lascaux-cave-paintings

Chugani, G. (2016, March 14). Harsha. World History Encyclopedia. https://www.worldhistory.org/Harsha/

Cookson, E., Hill, D. J., & Lawrence, D. (2019). Impacts of Long Term Climate Change During the Collapse of the Akkadian Empire. Journal of Archaeological Science, 106(0305-4403), 1–9. https://doi.org/10.1016/j.jas.2019.03.009

Dabholkar, V. (2014, January 4). Killing an Idea: Lessons from the Destruction of Nalanda University. Catalign Innovation Consulting. https://www.catalign.in/2014/01/killing-idea-lessons-from-destruction.html

Decline of the Indus River Valley Civilization (c. 3300-1300 BCE). (n.d.). Climate in Arts and History. https://www.science.smith.edu/climatelit/decline-of-the-indus-river-valley-civilization-c-3300-1300-bce/

DHWTY. (2021, February 3). Remembering Harsha: The Forgotten Vardhana Ruler of India. Ancient Origins . https://www.ancient-origins.net/history-famous-people/harsha-0014882

Duffy, J. (2022, July 2). A Complete Guide to Norse Gods & Goddesses. Panorama Glass Lodge. https://panoramaglasslodge.com/a-complete-guide-to-norse-gods-goddesses/

Eames, C. (2018, November 11). Nebuchadnezzar's "Tower of Babel." Armstrong Institute of Biblical Archaeology. https://armstronginstitute.org/125-nebuchadnezzars-tower-of-babel

Eduljee, K. E. (n.d.). Persepolis. Zoroastrian Heritage. https://www.heritageinstitute.com/zoroastrianism/persepolis/destruction.htm

Fox, A. (2020, July 2). Why Did the Maya Abandon the Ancient City of Tikal? Smithsonian Magazine. https://www.smithsonianmag.com/smart-news/maya-abandoned-city-tikal-researchers-may-now-know-why-180975242/

Fox, I. (2020, June 21). The Pharaoh's Curse? — The Tale of Tutankhamun's Trumpets... 4barsrest. https://www.4barsrest.com/articles/2020/1881.asp

Friðriksdóttir, J. K. (2022, February 25). Christians and Pagans in Norse Society: The Real Religious Rifts between Vikings. History Extra. https://www.historyextra.com/period/viking/viking-christianity-christians-pagans-norse-society-religious-conflict/

Gannon, M. (2017, December 27). China's First Emperor Ordered Official Search for Immortality Elixir. Live Science. https://www.livescience.com/61286-first-chinese-emperor-sought-immortality.html

Groeneveld, E. (2018, November 12). Ivar the Boneless. World History Encyclopedia. https://www.worldhistory.org/Ivar_the_Boneless/

Harsha - Facts about King Harshavardhana [NCERT Notes on Ancient Indian History For UPSC]. (n.d.). BYJU'S Exam Prep. https://byjus.com/free-ias-prep/ncert-notes-king-harshavardhana/

Pyramid of Dahshur. ThoughtCo. https://www.thoughtco.com/bent-pyramid-of-dahshur-170220

Hirst, K. K. (2019, October 6). Biography of Ivar the Boneless, Ragnar Lodbrok's Son. ThoughtCo. https://www.thoughtco.com/ivar-the-boneless-4771437

History and Revival. (2019). Nalanda University. https://nalandauniv.edu.in/about-nalanda/history-and-revival/

History Skills. (n.d.-a). 13 of the Weirdest Facts about King Tutankhamun. History Skills. https://www.historyskills.com/classroom/year-7/weird-facts-about-king-tut/

History.com Editors. (2009a, November 9). Nero. HISTORY. https://www.history.com/topics/ancient-rome/nero

History.com Editors. (2009b, November 24). Lascaux Cave Paintings Discovered. HISTORY. https://www.history.com/this-day-in-history/lascaux-cave-paintings-discovered/

History.com Editors. (2023, July 13). Battle of Marathon. HISTORY. https://www.history.com/topics/ancient-greece/battle-of-marathon/

Ivar Ragnarsson. (2023, October 22). Viking Heritage. https://www.vikingheritage.net/blogs/viking/ivar-ragnarsson

Kumar, R. (2017, September 11). Nalanda: 9 Million Books Burnt in 1193 by Bakhtiyar Khilji. My India My Glory. https://www.myindiamyglory.com/2017/09/11/nalanda-9-million-books-burnt/

Lal, A. (2019, June 5). Pushyabhuti Dynasty. World History Encyclopedia. https://www.worldhistory.org/Pushyabhuti_Dynasty/

Mark, J. J. (2019, November 26). Persian Immortals. World History Encyclopedia. https://www.worldhistory.org/Persian_Immortals/

Milligan, M. (2020, June 3). Mohenjo-Daro – Mound of the Dead Men. Heritage Daily. https://www.heritagedaily.com/2020/06/mohenjo-daro-mound-of-the-dead-men/129711

Ms Elly. (2019, March 9). Which Viking Found America First, Leif Eríksson or Bjarni Herjólfsson? BaVi. https://bavipower.com/blogs/bavipower-viking-blog/which-viking-found-america-first

Muench, S. (2013, September 16). Colosseum. Engineering Rome. https://engineeringrome.org/colosseum/

Mukherjee, S. (2023, February 23). Nalanda: The University that Changed the World. BBC. https://www.bbc.com/travel/article/20230222-nalanda-the-university-that-changed-the-world

Nalanda University During Harsha`s Reign. (n.d.). India Netzone. https://www.indianetzone.com/25/nalanda_during_harsha_s_reign.htm

National Museum of Denmark. (2019). Christianity Comes to Denmark . National Museum of Denmark. https://en.natmus.dk/historical-knowledge/denmark/prehistoric-period-until-1050-ad/the-viking-age/religion-magic-death-and-rituals/christianity-comes-to-denmark/

Oliver, M. (2022, August 20). How Ivar the Boneless Became One of History's Most Feared Vikings (J. Kuroski, Ed.). All That's Interesting. https://allthatsinteresting.com/ivar-the-boneless

Pillalamarri, A. (2016, June 2). Revealed: The Truth Behind the Indus Valley Civilization's "Collapse." The Diplomat. https://thediplomat.com/2016/06/revealed-the-truth-behind-the-indus-valley-civilizations-collapse/

Rongmei, P. (2023, March 8). All You Need to Know about Nalanda University, a Remarkable Centre of Learning. Times Travel. https://timesofindia.indiatimes.com/travel/destinations/all-you-need-to-know-about-nalanda-university-a-remarkable-centre-of-learning/articleshow/98495100.cms

Rybachuk, M. (2023, August 14). Aeschylus, the Father of Greek Tragedy Who Met an Absurd Death. Greek Reporter. https://greekreporter.com/2023/08/14/aeschylus-greek-tragedy-death/

Salem, C. (2023, February 26). Borsippa: Exploring the Magnificent City of the Ancient Babylonian Ziggurat. Nineveh Rising. https://www.ninevehrising.org/post/borsippa-exploring-the-magnificent-city-of-the-ancient-babylonian-ziggurat

Scharping, N. (2020, November 7). Did the Great Wall of China Actually Keep Invaders Out? Discover. https://www.discovermagazine.com/uncategorized/did-the-great-wall-of-china-actually-keep-invaders-out

Schuman, M. (2019, January 20). Opinion: China Built a Big, Beautiful Wall, Too. Why It Failed. The Morning Call. https://www.mcall.com/2019/01/20/opinion-china-built-a-big-beautiful-wall-too-why-it-failed/

Seven of the Most Important Gods and Goddesses in Norse Mythology. (n.d.). Sky HISTORY . https://www.history.co.uk/articles/seven-of-the-most-important-gods-and-goddesses-in-norse-mythology

Sicilian Expedition. (2005). Livius.org. https://www.livius.org/articles/concept/peloponnesian-war/sicilian-expedition/

Taronas, L. (n.d.). Nefertiti: Egyptian Wife, Mother, Queen and Icon. ARCE. https://arce.org/resource/nefertiti-egyptian-wife-mother-queen-and-icon/

The Gods of the Old Nordic Religion. (2019). National Museum of Denmark. https://en.natmus.dk/historical-knowledge/denmark/prehistoric-period-until-1050-ad/the-viking-age/religion-magic-death-and-rituals/the-viking-gods/

The Great Wall of China. (n.d.). The Great Wall of China. https://web.cortland.edu/wangh/project1/wall.htm

The Vinland Sagas: The Men Who Discovered America before Columbus. (2017, November 17). Interesting Literature. https://interestingliterature.com/2017/11/the-vinland-sagas-the-men-who-discovered-america-before-columbus/

Venegas, R. (n.d.). Wars Between Calakmul and Tikal. Historical Mexico. https://historicalmx.org/items/show/81

Vikings: From Pagans to Christians; How Did It Happen? (2018, May 29). History on the Net. https://www.historyonthenet.com/vikings-from-pagans-to-christians

Why Did the Vikings Leave North America? (2021, April 9). History in Charts. https://historyincharts.com/the-history-of-the-vikings-in-the-americas/

Wilkinson, T. (2022, December 8). The Pharaoh's Trumpet (P. Weintraub, Ed.). Aeon. https://aeon.co/essays/what-king-tuts-treasures-reveal-about-daily-life-in-ancient-egypt

Wilson, M. (2013, July 24). Destroying a Temple. Biblical Archaeology Society. https://www.biblicalarchaeology.org/daily/biblical-sites-places/biblical-archaeology-sites/destroying-a-temple

Winston, A. (n.d.). The Pyramid of Snefru (Bent Pyramid) at Dahshur. Tour Egypt. https://www.touregypt.net/featurestories/snefrubentp.htm

Zhu, M. (2019). The Grand Canal . Environmental China. https://environmentalchina.history.lmu.build/group-page-theme-2-water-control/the-grand-canal/

Made in the USA
Las Vegas, NV
21 April 2024

88962479R00069